The Way to Pass
English
Level 6

The Way to Pass National Curriculum English
Level 6

Brian Keaney

VERMILION
LONDON

First published in 1994

1 3 5 7 9 10 8 6 4 2

Text copyright © Rockhopper 1994

The moral right of the Author has been asserted in accordance with the Copyright, Designs and Patents Act, 1988.

All rights reserved. No part of this publication may be reproduced, stored in a retrieval system, or transmitted in any form or by any means, electronic, mechanical, photocopying, recording or otherwise, without the prior permission of the copyright owner.

First published in the United Kingdom in 1994 by Vermilion
an imprint of Ebury Press
Random House, 20 Vauxhall Bridge Road, London SW1V 2SA

Random House Australia (Pty) Limited
20 Alfred Street, Milsons Point, Sydney, New South Wales 2061, Australia

Random House New Zealand Limited
18 Poland Road, Glenfield,
Auckland 10, New Zealand

Random House South Africa (Pty) Limited
PO Box 337, Bergvlei, South Africa

Random House UK Limited Reg. No. 954009

Editor: Alison Wormleighton
Design: Jerry Goldie Graphic Design

A CIP catalogue record for this book is available from the British Library

ISBN 0-09-178133-7

Typeset by Textype Typesetters, Cambridge
Printed in Great Britain by Butler & Tanner, Ltd., London and Frome

Foreword

Welcome to THE WAY TO PASS NATIONAL CURRICULUM ENGLISH LEVEL 6. I want to tell you why I have put this series of books together, along with a team of teachers, advisers and examiners.

There are many wonderful and enjoyable aspects involved with studying English, but sometimes it's important to focus on the precise things which we need to learn and understand. It's only by doing this that you can know how to improve your grades in your coursework and exams.

Whatever you might think about school, and about English in particular, there is no doubt that English and Maths are the two most important subjects for you to do well in. If you understand what you're taught, you are set for a brighter future, being able to do some of the things you've always wanted to.

THE WAY TO PASS series can help you through secondary school, making the subjects you're taught a little more understandable and interesting, making your tests easier, and helping you to get the best grades possible. The books are based on work for you to do at home so you can revise at your own pace, concentrating on the areas in which you feel you need help.

This completely new range of books has been organised so that, if you want to, you can follow the already successful VIDEO CLASS videos covering the same subjects. All of the book sections work together neatly with the video sections so that you have a complete course at your fingertips. Alternatively, the books can be used on their own, without the videos.

I certainly hope that this series will make English and Maths more approachable and slightly friendlier than they were before. Remember, you must follow what is taught in school and do as many exercises as you can – the more practice you get, the better you will be.

Carol Vorderman

Contents

The National Curriculum 8
Introduction 9

1 The Changing Face of English — 10
   Skills You Need — 10
   Improving Your Skills — 10
      Our literary heritage — 10
      Creating language — 16
      Understanding register — 17
   Do It Yourself — 19

2 The Language of Persuasion — 24
   Skills You Need — 24
   Improving Your Skills — 24
      Levels of meaning — 24
      Manipulating language — 27
      Getting your point across — 28
   Do It Yourself — 30

3 Effective Communication — 33
   Skills You Need — 33
   Improving Your Skills — 33
      Formal and informal groups — 34
      A class discussion — 38
      One-to-one — 40
      Presenting a talk — 42
   Do It Yourself — 43

4 Researching and Reporting   46
- Skills You Need   46
- Improving Your Skills   46
  - Researching   47
  - Writing reports   51
  - Writing narrative   55
  - Reported speech   56
- Do It Yourself   59

5 Using a Library   61
- Skills You Need   61
- Improving Your Skills   61
  - How a library works   61
  - Choosing books   63
  - Creating a reading programme   65
- Do It Yourself   69

6 Tools for English   73
- Parts of Speech   73
- Sentence grammar   78
- Spelling   79
- Punctuation   84
- Do It Yourself   88

Answers   90
Index   107

The National Curriculum

The National Curriculum sets targets for pupils of all abilities from age 5 to 16, specifying what they should know, understand and be able to do at each stage of their education. It is divided into four **Key Stages**: Key Stage 1 (age 5–7), Key Stage 2 (age 7–11), Key Stage 3 (age 11–14) and Key Stage 4 (age 14–16).

The GCSE examinations are the main way of assessing children's progress at the end of Key Stage 4 (age 16). Prior to that, at the end of Key Stages 1, 2 and 3 (i.e. at ages 7, 11 and 14), pupils will be assessed in two ways: continuous assessment by the teachers and national tests, in which children will be asked to perform specific tasks relevant to the subject. Children will take the tests in English and Maths at age 7, 11 and 14 and in Science at age 11 and 14. These three subjects are at the heart of the National Curriculum and are known as the **core subjects**.

By combining the test results and continuous assessment, a teacher will be able to determine the **Level** a child has reached in each of these subjects. Different children at the same Key Stage may achieve widely varying results and therefore different Levels.

An average child will probably move up one Level every two years or so, starting at Level 1 at the age of 5. This means that at the end of Key Stage 1 (age 7) they may reach Level 2, at the end of Key Stage 2 (age 11) Level 4 and at the end of Key Stage 3 (age 14) Level 5 or 6. Slower learners could be a level or two lower in one or more subjects, while some children could be two or even three Levels higher. Level 10 is the highest, but only a few children will achieve this Level.

The books for Levels 4, 5 and 6 in THE WAY TO PASS series are based on National Curriculum requirements for each of those Levels and are suitable for the secondary school child aged 11 to 14. They will serve as a valuable back-up to a child's classwork and homework and provide an excellent preparation for the tests at the end of Key Stage 3.

Introduction

This book is called THE WAY TO PASS NATIONAL CURRICULUM ENGLISH LEVEL 6, but it's much more than that. When you've finished working through it, you'll find that you've learned and polished a number of skills which you need, not just to pass tests and exams at school, but in everyday life as well.

For you, English is both work and a means of communication. It's important at school because it's the language you speak, read and write every day of your life. If you want to be able to say *exactly* what you want, think, do, feel, hope, etc., as well as get the most out of what you read, you must learn how to use and understand your own language.

English is the basis for *all* your school work: you use it to talk and write about your other subjects. So it's worth widening your vocabulary, improving your spelling and writing, speaking with greater confidence and deepening your understanding. You'll also find that you communicate more easily with your family, friends and other people.

This book aims to help you to improve and develop these skills, especially those you need for Level 6 English. Each of the five sections looks at one or more of the National Curriculum requirements, and there are three help lines in each section to guide you:

- **Skills You Need** to tell you what skills you should have;
- **Improving Your Skills** to give you more information about those skills, and some examples of the tasks where you need to use them; and
- **Do It Yourself** to give you the chance to practise your skills.

Use the **Tools for English** section either for reference or to check your understanding by doing the exercises.

In the final part, **Answers**, you will find answers or suggestions for many, but not all, of the Do It Yourself activities. English is not a subject where answers are always right or wrong.

Remember, with this book you can do whatever English activity you like, in any order, and whenever you like. Enjoy your English, because that is the way to succeed!

SECTION 1

The Changing Face of English

CONTENTS

Our literary heritage

❖

Creating language

❖

Understanding register

'English is always changing. Our language is alive.'

Skills You Need

You need to be able to:
- understand the nature and extent of language change
- respond to the language of a text written before the twentieth century
- show understanding and appropriate use of language register

Improving Your Skills

People have been writing books in English for hundreds of years. The English language has one of the richest literary heritages in the world.

Our literary heritage

If we try to read a book by Geoffrey Chaucer, who lived six hundred years ago, William Shakespeare, who lived four hundred years ago, or even a relative newcomer like Oscar Wilde, who died at the beginning of this century, we often find the language difficult to understand.

The reason for this is not, as some people suppose, because writers like this are 'hard'. It is just that language changes all the time. It changes because we want it to. After all, language is a tool for communication. Just as human beings changed from using stone tools to using ones made from iron and steel, so, too, language, the communication tool, evolved to deal with the increasingly complex demands that were made upon it.

This does not mean that the plays of Shakespeare, for example, are less sophisticated than the writings of modern authors. Many people would say that Shakespeare's works are the greatest literature that has ever been written in the English language. It does mean, however, that the language in which Shakespeare wrote is different from the language writers used before and after him.

The evolution of English

When we are learning another language, we often notice similarities between some of the words in that language and English words. Sometimes the reason for this is obvious. Perhaps one language has borrowed words from another. We do this all the time when we discover new kinds of food. For example, *curry*, *pizza*, *goulash*, *hamburger* and *bagel* are all borrowed from the countries in which these dishes were first eaten.

Language families

The similarities can also go much deeper than this. If we look closely at languages we begin to see patterns. This is because languages come in families, and inside any one family there are always similarities. English is part of the Indo-European family. Its relatives include Latin, Bengali, Hindi, Urdu, Russian, Polish, French, German, Welsh, Gaelic, Greek and Swedish.

A language group like this is called a *family* because all the members have the same ancestors. The oldest ancestor in the Indo-European group is an ancient, unwritten language called Proto-Indo-European, which we believe was spoken by people in the area which is now Southern Russian and Poland about seven thousand years ago.

These people travelled, and as they did so they took their language with them. Gradually their language changed as the people moved further from their starting place. Some went to Northern India, some to Russia, while others went west across Europe, and it is from this last group that the languages spoken by most people in Europe have evolved.

However, not every language in Europe is a part of the Indo-European family. Finnish, Hungarian and Turkish are in a family all of their own, and in one tiny corner of Spain, the Basque country, people speak a language whose origin is entirely unknown.

SECTION 1
IMPROVING YOUR SKILLS

'Why does language change? Because we want it to.'

THE CHANGING FACE OF ENGLISH
IMPROVING YOUR SKILLS

'Don't assume that every language in Europe is Indo-European.'

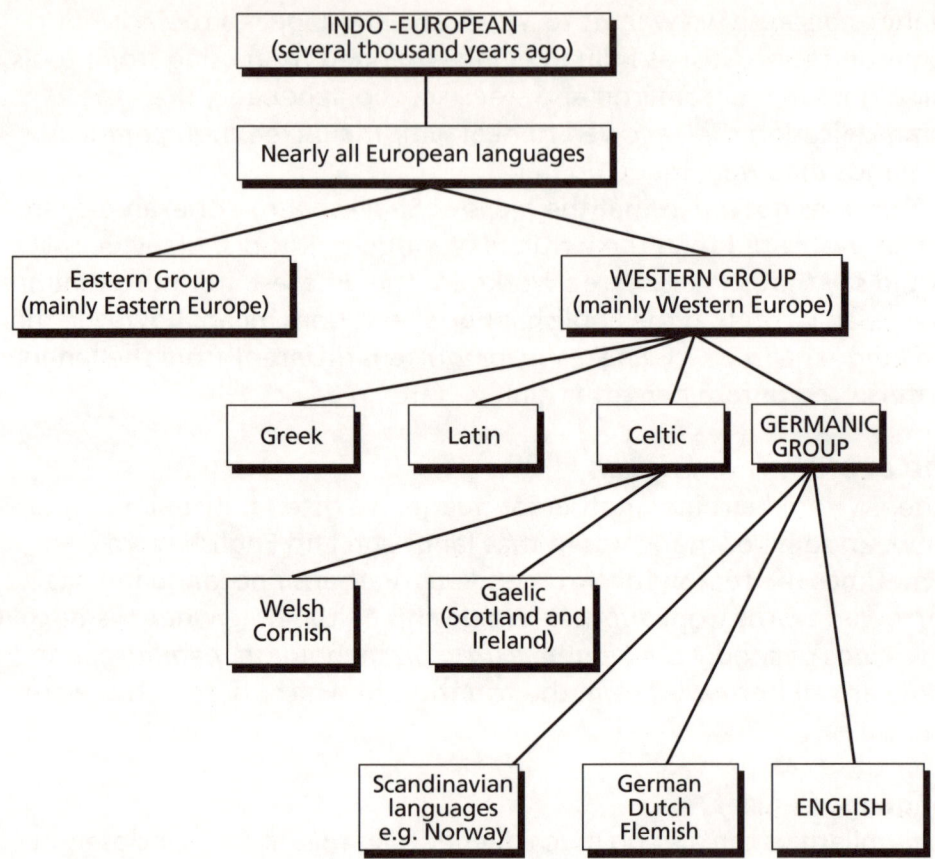

Latin and Greek influences

The influence of Latin and Greek on our language has been enormous. We call these languages *classical* and we still use the word *classic* to mean something that is excellent or has survived the test of time. These classical languages came into the English language in a number of different ways, and as a result many words in English have Latin roots.

Latin was the language spoken by the Romans, who conquered Britain in AD 43 and made it part of the Roman Empire. Very few words actually survive from that time, however.

The language of the Christian church was Latin and, as Christianity spread over much of the world, so did Latin. Many words connected with the church date from this time (the 7th century).

The Normans, who conquered Britain in 1066, used Latin in official business and church services, and French in everyday life. French is one of the Italic, or Romance, languages, all of which developed from Latin.

SECTION 1
IMPROVING YOUR SKILLS

Many words that originated as Latin words came into the English language through French.

The following list shows some of these English words with the Latin words from which they originated via French.

Modern English	Latin
maternal	maternus
descend	descendere
imbibe	imbibere
elevated	elevare
miserable	miser
accelerate	accelerare
observe	observare
detest	detestari
repeat	repetere

'All languages are thieves – they borrow from each other.'

During the Middle Ages, Latin was spoken alongside French and English. Then, during the Renaissance – when Europeans rediscovered Greek and Roman culture and consciously copied Greek and Roman art, ideas and words – many new words of Latin origin came into English, such as *benefit, consolidate, exert, exhilarated, exist, extinguish, mediate*.

The Romans had themselves been highly influenced by the Ancient Greeks, who had a civilisation and a language older than those of Rome. The Ancient Greeks used a different set of letters than we do. Their set of letters was the first in which every letter stood for a sound. (Previously people had used *pictograms* – letters representing whole words or ideas. The hieroglyphs of Ancient Egypt are examples of pictograms.) Greek words entered the English language through Ancient Greek books which were brought to Europe from libraries at Constantinople and Alexandria during the Middle Ages and the Renaissance.

The Greeks were great thinkers and philosophers. They were the first to divide knowledge up into different areas and to give each of these areas a name of its own. Many of the words that we use for the subjects we study – such as *history* and *arithmetic* (from the Greek *historia* and *arithmos*, meaning 'inquiry' and 'number') – were originally Greek words. Because the Greek language included words for different kinds of knowledge, it has often been used to make new words for scientific discoveries and inventions.

Time to go back to your roots! Find the Latin basis for each English word in Do It Yourself Exercise 1, on page 19.

Old English
The original inhabitants of England spoke Celtic languages. Then they were invaded by tribes from Northern Europe, called the Angles, the

13

THE CHANGING FACE OF ENGLISH
IMPROVING YOUR SKILLS

Saxons and the Jutes. The Celts were driven out of the centre of England into Wales, Scotland and Cornwall and across the sea to Ireland. In most of these places Celtic languages are still spoken.

The new inhabitants of England spoke a language which we call Old English or Anglo-Saxon. The writings which have survived from this time look very strange to us now. For example, look at the first line of the Lord's Prayer, or Our Father, as they would have written it:

Faeder ure þu þe eart on heofonum

The letter þ was known as 'thorn' and pronounced *th*. It stopped being used a very long time ago, though it is still sometimes seen in signs like 'Ye Olde English Tea Shoppe' where the Y really stands for a badly made þ.

Shown below are some examples of English words derived from Anglo-Saxon words.

Modern English	Anglo-Saxon
mother	modor
go down	gan
drink	drincan
high	heah
sad	saed
speed	spowan
watch	waeccan
hate	hete
do again	don ongean

Middle English

Old English changed dramatically when England was conquered by the Normans in the eleventh century. The Normans spoke French, and even after coming to live in England they continued to use their own language. At first the two languages, Norman French and the Old English of the Anglo-Saxons, were very separate. You can still see a good example of this if you look at the words that we use for meat.

The Normans were the rulers and they enjoyed a good lifestyle, eating plenty of meat. So the words we have for different kinds of meat are borrowed from the French.

Modern English	French
beef	boeuf
pork	porc
mutton	mouton

'Usually the country that is best at a certain activity supplies the words for the other countries.'

SECTION 1

IMPROVING YOUR SKILLS

It was the peasants, however, who looked after the animals, even if they could not afford to eat them, and they continued to use the Old English names for them: cow, pig, sheep. As a result, we now have separate names for the animals themselves and the meat which they produce.

As time passed, the two classes, the rulers and the peasants, began to come closer together. Trade and intermarriage played their part. The two languages gradually began to merge into one. A new English was born, which we now call Middle English. It was enriched by a French vocabulary and it was simplified, too. Nevertheless, it was still very different from the language we use today.

The greatest writer of the Middle English period was Geoffrey Chaucer. Look at how he begins his most famous poem, *The Canterbury Tales*.

> Whan that Aprill with his shoures soote
> The droghte of March hath perced to the roote

How much of it can you understand? Here is a modern translation.

> *When the sweet showers of April*
> *Have put an end to the drought of March*

It is not just the words that have changed. Some of the grammar rules have changed also. Chaucer could use double or even treble negatives, as in this description of a good man:

> *He never yet no vileinye ne said.*

However, if someone nowadays were to say

> I never done no one no harm

we would say that they were not speaking Standard English.

Shakespeare's English
It is still a long way from Chaucer's English to the language that we speak nowadays. Shakespeare wrote his plays two hundred years after Chaucer, but they can still present us with difficulties in understanding. When Juliet leans out of the balcony in *Romeo and Juliet*, and asks

> 'Romeo, Romeo, wherefore art thou Romeo?'

she is not asking where he is, as some people suppose. The word 'wherefore' meant *why*. She is wishing he was someone else and not a member of the family that is involved in a feud with her own. She is asking:

> 'Romeo, Romeo, why did you have to be Romeo?'

> **'In Standard English, a double negative is considered to be "bad grammar".'**

To compare Shakespeare's English with a 'simplified' version of it, turn to Do It Yourself Exercises 2 and 3 on pages 20–22.

THE CHANGING FACE OF ENGLISH
IMPROVING YOUR SKILLS

> *'A language dies when people find it more useful to speak something else.'*

Modern English
In modern times communication has been the greatest factor in the way that language has changed. We are able to see so many new things on television, read about events as they happen, sample other people's cultures. New words have been coined (created) to describe new inventions or ideas. Often these words are made up using Latin or Ancient Greek words. These two languages are sometimes described as 'dead'. This means that no one speaks them, except for scholars. As a result we can easily take words from them to make new words for our own language. For example, photograph comes from two Greek words meaning 'light' and 'to write'. Computer comes from a Latin word meaning 'to calculate'.

We have also taken words from other languages and from phrases used in the entertainment world or in politics. Celebrities have created new fashions; new jokes have been made about new events – all these things have added to the richness of our vocabulary.

English is now used as second language by a huge number of people throughout the world. People in countries everywhere are speaking and writing it. We pick up each other's phrases and sayings. Interests, like music, are shared by people from very different cultures who swop vocabulary, ideas and stories all the time.

> *'Words change for a whole lot of reasons.'*

Creating language
The English language is being created all the time all over the world. This is because the human brain is a creative tool. We come up with ways of saying things which please us, are useful or fulfil a new need, and they stick in our language.

Idioms
One of the most interesting ways in which we use our language is in making up idioms. Idioms are ways of saying things indirectly, by creating word-pictures. It is done by people all the time, particularly in spoken language.

For example, we talk about people being 'round the bend' when we mean they are mad or angry. When we describe sports personalities as 'over the hill' we imply that they are getting too old to compete. These idiomatic expressions are a distinguishing feature of a native speaker, and are very difficult to acquire for people who are learning English as their second language.

Every language has its own idioms and, though they are sometimes surprisingly alike, they are seldom identical. In England, people sometimes say that someone has got 'egg on their face', meaning that they look rather foolish because of something they have done. In Germany, they talk about 'having tomatoes in front of your eyes' when you can't see something that is right in front of you.

Euphemisms

When we are embarrassed about something, or when we are worried that we might offend someone, we sometimes use a special kind of idiom, known as a euphemism.

For example, instead of talking about someone dying, we may say that they have 'passed away'. Death is one of the subjects that people often prefer not to talk about. Another is using the lavatory, which is sometimes described as 'spending a penny' or 'paying a visit'.

Would you spot a euphemism if you heard or saw it? Would you know what was meant? See if you can explain those in Exercise 4 on page 23 of Do It Yourself.

Slang

Slang is the deliberate invention of an alternative non-Standard word or phrase to describe something. The expression 'wannabe' is an example of slang. 'Wannabe' was a word first coined in the 1980s to describe a fan who wanted to be like their idol – a wannabe Madonna, for example.

Today's slang is often perfectly acceptable. 'Wannabe' is now in the *Oxford English Dictionary* and is frequently used by journalists. This is another way in which language changes.

'*Slang words change according to the fashion.*'

Acronyms

Words are also made up from other words. When we want to use the name of an organisation, or an invention, or an illness, for example, that is made up of a number of other words, we often just use the initial letters. We would say Nato rather than the North Atlantic Treaty Organisation, the UN instead of the United Nations, or Aids instead of Acquired Immune Deficiency Syndrome. Words formed from the initial letters of other words are called *acronyms*. Sometimes these are written as capital letters, usually when the letters are pronounced individually, like U-N (not 'un').

Eponyms

Another way in which we acquire new words is from people's names. Inventions are often named after their inventors, such as 'sandwich', which we get from the Earl of Sandwich, who did not want to interrupt a gambling game and asked for a snack he could eat while playing, or 'biro', named after Ladislao Biro, the Hungarian artist who developed it.

Would you recognise an inventor from his eponym? Try your luck with Exercise 5 on page 23 of Do It Yourself.

THE CHANGING FACE OF ENGLISH
IMPROVING YOUR SKILLS

How is your geography? Where do the words in Exercise 6 of Do It Yourself come from? (You'll find them on page 23.)

Toponyms

Words which are formed because of their association with places are called *toponyms*. For example, jersey is the name for a garment originally made of wool from the island of Jersey, while the word 'denim' derived from *'de Nîmes'*, which is French for 'from Nîmes', the town where the fabric was first made.

Understanding register

When you use a euphemism you are making a language choice. For example, if we were comforting someone whose friend or loved one had died, we might decide to say that the person had 'passed on'. On the other hand we might decide that this did not sound sincere.

Making a decision about how to express something is a part of the process of choosing the right *register,* or form of language. We use different registers for different occasions, depending on how formal or informal, how friendly or polite we want to sound, and whether we are talking to people older or younger than ourselves, members of our family, friends or people we feel nervous around.

Of course, we do not usually start every conversation by thinking long and hard about the most suitable register to adopt. If we did this, most of us would hardly say anything at all. It is something we do naturally, like smiling at people or looking concerned.

For practice in choosing the appropriate register, turn to Do It Yourself Exercise 7 on page 23.

However, there are times when we like to be especially careful about what we say and how we say it, like in an important interview, for example. There are times, too, when we get it wrong, sound too casual and give out the wrong signals.

Dialect and accent

Register is not the same thing as dialect and accent. Dialect is a set of words and phrases which are used by people from a particular area or by members of a particular ethnic or cultural group living within a predominant culture. It also includes the rules for putting those words and phrases together.

For example, in a part of Northern Ireland there is a tendency to put the word 'but' at the end of a sentence, rather than in the middle. Someone who speaks like this might say:

> 'I would go back, there's no one at home but.'

To people not brought up in that area, this seems very strange. It is simply a dialect usage and is not recognised as Standard English.

SECTION 1
DO IT YOURSELF

Standard English

We pick up language register gradually – by studying, listening and reading – learning what kinds of words and grammar are appropriate with which people and in what situation.

However, when it comes to writing things down, people would not easily understand if we wrote in dialect, which is why we use Standard English. It can be used with a variety of *accents* – for example, someone who has a Japanese accent can speak Standard English, as can someone with a Nigerian accent, or a Yorkshire accent, as long as the vocabulary and grammar (the words spoken and the rules which determine how they are put together) are standard.

Your accent is simply the way you speak, the music of your language. For example, people in the North of England pronounce the word *bath* quite differently from people in the South, while people in Scotland pronounce *-ch* quite differently from people in Cornwall.

Standardisation slows down the process of change. If this were not so, the English spoken in countries like Australia, America or India might by now have become so different that they would have become languages in their own right, like the languages of the Indo-Europeans.

Do It Yourself

Activities marked with a * have answers, or suggested answers, in the Answers section at the back of the book.

You may need the help of a dictionary or encyclopaedia.

1 * How many English words can you find which have been made from the following Latin roots?

(a)	scrib-	(from *scribo, scriptum,* write)
(b)	duct-	(from *duco, ductum,* lead)
(c)	pon-, posit-	(from *pono, positum,* place)
(d)	cred-	(from *credo, creditum,* believe)
(e)	solv-	(from *solvo, solutum,* dissolve)
(f)	dict-	(from *dico, dictum,* say)
(g)	capio-, cept-	(from *capio, captum,* take)
(h)	ject-	(from *iacio, iactum,* throw)
(i)	ced-, cess-	(from *cedo, cessum,* go)
(j)	ag-, act-	(from *ago, actum,* act or do)
(k)	curr-	(from *curro, cursum,* run)

'Writing slows down language change.'

'Accent is the way we pronounce our words – the rhythms and sounds of our speech.'

'Sometimes we can guess the meanings of words because they are similar to our own.'

THE CHANGING FACE OF ENGLISH
DO IT YOURSELF

2 * Read the following extract from *Macbeth* by William Shakespeare and answer the questions that follow. In it, three witches meet. One of them has been offended by a woman, and the witch plans to get her revenge on the woman's husband.

Macbeth
Act 3, Scene III. [A heath.]

Thunder. Enter the Three Witches

First Witch. *Where hast thou been, sister?*

Second Witch. *Killing swine.*

Third Witch. *Sister, where thou?*

First Witch. *A sailor's wife had chestnuts in her lap,*
   And mounched, and mounched, and mounched.
     'Give me,' quoth I.   5
   'Aroint thee,°witch!' the rump-fed ronyon° cries.
   Her husband's to Aleppo gone, master o' th' Tiger:
   But in a sieve I'll thither sail,
   And, like a rat without a tail,
   I'll do, I'll do, and I'll do.   10

Second Witch. *I'll give thee a wind.*

First Witch. *Th' art kind.*

Third Witch. *And I another.*

First Witch. *I myself have all the other;*
   And the very ports they blow,°   15
   All the quarters that they know
   I' th' shipman's card.°
   I'll drain him dry as hay:
   Sleep shall neither night nor day
   Hang upon his penthouse lid;°   20
   He shall live a man forbid:°
   Weary sev'nights nine times nine
   Shall he dwindle, peak,° and pine:
   Though his bark° cannot be lost,
   Yet it shall be tempest-tossed.   25
   Look what I have.

Second Witch. *Show me, show me.*

First Witch. *Here I have a pilot's thumb,*
   Wracked as homeward he did come.

            Drum within.

SECTION 1
DO IT YOURSELF

  Third Witch. *A drum, a drum!*   30
   Macbeth doth come.
  All. *The weïrd° sisters, hand in hand,*
   Posters° of the sea and land,
   Thus do go about, about:
   Thrice to thine, and thrice to mine,   35
   And thrice again, to make up nine.
   Peace! The charm's wound up.

Notes °

aroint thee	begone
ronyon	scabby creature
ports they blow	the ports they blow to or visit
I' th' shipman's card	on the sailor's chart
penthouse lid	eyelid
forbid	cursed
peak	waste away
barkship	
weïrd	destiny-serving
posters	swift travellers

(a) What had the First Witch been doing before meeting the others?
(b) What did the woman do and say which annoyed the witch?
(c) What was the name of her husband's ship?
(d) Say one way in which each of the other two witches offered to help.
(e) What object does the First Witch use in her spell?
(f) What will be the effect of the spell on the sailor?
(g) What will its effect be on his boat?
(h) Why are they called 'posters of the sea and land'?
(i) In the last six lines of this extract the witches cast their spell. How does the language change to show this?
(j) What action do the witches perform to seal the spell?

3 * Nearly two hundred years after Shakespeare wrote his plays, two writers, Charles and Mary Lamb, published their book *Tales from Shakespeare*. It was intended to tell the stories of Shakespeare's plays in language that would be understood by the children of the day. Nearly two hundred more years have passed since the Lambs wrote their book, and *its* language now seems difficult to us.

THE CHANGING FACE OF ENGLISH
DO IT YOURSELF

Read the following passage from the Lambs' version of *As You Like It* and answer the questions that follow.

As You Like It

During the time that France was divided into provinces (or dukedoms, as they were called) there reigned in one of these provinces a usurper, who had deposed and banished his elder brother, the lawful duke.

The duke, who was thus driven from his dominions, retired with a few faithful followers to the forest of Arden; and here the good duke lived with his loving friends, who had put themselves into a voluntary exile for his sake, while their land and revenues enriched the false usurper; and custom soon made the life of careless ease they led here more sweet to them than the pomp and uneasy splendour of a courtier's life. Here they all lived like the old Robin Hood of England, and to this forest many noble youths daily resorted from the court, and did fleet the time carelessly, as they did who lived in the golden age. In the summer they lay along under the fine shade of the large forest trees, marking the playful sports of the wild deer; and so fond were they of these poor dappled fools, who seemed to be the native inhabitants of the forest, that it grieved them to be forced to kill them to supply themselves with venison for food. When the cold winds of winter made the duke feel the change of his adverse fortune, he would endure it patiently, and say, 'These chilling winds which blow upon my body are true counsellors: they do not flatter, but represent truly to me my condition; and though they bite sharply, their tooth is nothing like so keen as that of unkindness and ingratitude.'

(a) What is the meaning of the word 'usurper' in line 3?
(b) In your own words explain what the writers mean by saying that the duke's friends had 'put themselves into a voluntary exile for his sake'? (lines 7–8).
(c) Give another word or phrase for 'custom' (line 9).
(d) What do people usually mean when they say a 'golden age' (line 14)? What is the authors' idea of a golden age?
(e) Who are the 'poor dappled fools' (line 17)? Why are they poor?
(f) How did the duke's followers feel about killing deer for meat?
(g) In your own words explain the phrase 'when the cold winds of winter made the duke feel the change of his adverse fortune'.

SECTION 1

DO IT YOURSELF

4 * Explain in straightforward English what the following euphemisms mean:

one of Her Majesty's guests   a drop too much
gone to a better place   the smallest room
hard of hearing   invited to offer one's resignation
off colour   a little shy of the truth

'Sometimes we don't say exactly what we mean.'

5 * Can you find out the origins of these eponyms?

decibel   guillotine
boycott   diesel
mesmerise   chauvinist
pasteurise   hoover
tarmac   leotard

6 * Say what each of the following items is, and the place from which it gets its name.

panama   balaclava
duffel   muslin
bikini   jodhpurs
cashmere

7 Write one of the following, paying particular attention to your language choices:

(a) Form   a general letter
     Purpose/Audience   to be sent out to employers for whom you would like to work
     Subject   why I am worth employing
(b) Form   a leaflet
     Purpose/Audience   to be sent to all the students at your school
     Subject   what they can do to improve the school
(c) Form   a personal letter
     Purpose/Audience   to be sent to a friend
     Subject   why you cannot come to watch him/her performing

'Language register is something we pick up gradually over time.'

SECTION 2

The Language of Persuasion

CONTENTS

Levels of meaning

❖

Manipulating language

❖

Getting your point across

Skills You Need

You should be able to:
- consider meanings below the surface of a text
- tell the difference between fact and opinion
- understand the concepts of bias and objectivity
- recognise ambiguity

Improving Your Skills

Language enables people to communicate. It is a code for sending messages between people. These messages can take the form of greetings, jokes, advice, opinions, warnings, information and also advertisements.

Levels of meaning

Advertisement use words, and often images, in a deliberate attempt to influence individuals to buy a particular product. It is important to understand and analyse how advertisements work because they are such a significant part of our culture, and also because they affect the way

> *Language is used to influence people.*

the members of society behave. You need to be aware that they can be misleading. This may be because:

- they mean something different from what they appear to mean
- they make false claims
- they make claims that are too vague to prove
- they use emotive words and figures of speech
- they use images

Reading an advertisement is like reading any other text: the more you concentrate, the more you may see.

On the surface

At surface level, advertisements mean what they say. An advertisement which says 'prawn-flavoured crisps', means just that: the crisps have the taste of prawns. This does not necessarily mean that any prawns have been used in their manufacture, just a flavouring.

Ambiguity

The surface meaning of some advertisements can be quite difficult to understand. If someone describes a product as 'probably the best lager in the world', what do they really mean by the word *probably*? Similarly, if an advertisement says: 'Spel has more gleamingly white whites', its meaning remains uncertain. It is not clear what exactly it washes whiter *than*. We call this uncertainty of meaning *ambiguity*.

THE LANGUAGE OF PERSUASION
IMPROVING YOUR SKILLS

See if you can distinguish fact from opinion. There are some statements in Exercise 1 of Do It Yourself on page 30 for you to ponder over.

Fact and opinion

Advertisements may also sometimes blur the distinction between fact and opinion. A *fact* is something that has been demonstrated to be true. It is a fact that cows eat grass. An *opinion* is something which someone believes to be true, but with which others may disagree. It is an opinion that the seaside is the best place to go for a holiday.

Objectivity and bias

Advertisements generally provide information. An advertisement for a car might list statistics about the car: acceleration, fuel consumption, engine size and so on. However, it is important to remember that the people who compiled the information are not *objective* (neutral). They have an interest in selling you a car.

Because of their lack of objectivity, advertisers are likely to show bias in the statistics they give. *Bias* means favouring one side rather than another. Therefore, the advertiser might tell you good statistics about a car but not tell you some of the less favourable ones. In this case, the advertisement is biased.

'Opinion can be made to look like fact.'

Below the surface

Sometimes the hidden messages that an advertisement conveys can be even more important than the surface meaning. This is often done through images – pictures or dramas showing people in certain situations. People are shown reacting in certain ways that are either desirable or undesirable, because of a certain period.

A young man becomes much more attractive to women, or vice versa, because of the shampoo he or she uses, to give an example. This is a simplified description, and in fact most advertisers think very hard about the sort of image they want to create for their product, and the sort of image they want to suggest about those who use it.

A car advertiser may show a car driver smartly dressed. In this way he or she is creating an image of elegance which is associated, in the reader's or viewer's mind, with the car and the person who drives it.

People do not necessarily come away thinking, 'If I had a car like that, I would look elegant and stylish.' Most of us are not that easily fooled. However, if we see it often enough, the image may lodge in our minds and form a permanent association between the car in the advertisement and elegance and style. Another advertiser may present a more casual picture, if the idea is to associate the product with having a good time or relaxing.

People who make up advertisements are sometimes called the "hidden persuaders".

Advertisers also use images to blur the distinction between fact and opinion. If someone presenting us with statistical information is wearing a white coat and spectacles, we might find ourselves taking them more seriously, because we associate this sort of dress with scientists and facts.

Advertisers are always thinking about images and we should be aware of the way they use them to manipulate consumers.

Would you be taken in by the 'hidden persuaders'? Find out by doing Exercise 2 on page 30 of Do It Yourself.

Associations

One of the ways in which advertisers create their images is by using words which have associations for the reader, viewer or listener. The English language has a very rich and varied vocabulary, as we have already seen, and there are many words which are similar in meaning but which have quite different associations.

THE LANGUAGE OF PERSUASION
IMPROVING YOUR SKILLS

For practice in recognising subtle differences between words with similar meanings, turn to Do It Yourself Exercise 3, on page 30.

Look at the following lists. The words in the first column all have pleasant, positive associations. Those in the second column, although quite similar in meaning, have unpleasant, negative associations.

Positive associations	Negative associations
guard	conceal
gift	bribe
brave	reckless
reserved	shy
petite	short
scholar	bookworm

Manipulating language

The people who write advertisements are not unlike poets; both choose their words very carefully. Poets want every word of their poems to carry as much meaning as possible and to affect the audience as much as possible. Making advertisements for today's sophisticated media can cost huge amounts of money, and so the people who are selling the product do not want to get one word wrong, or use one more word than they have to.

Figures of speech

Like poets, advertisers use a variety of *devices* or *figures of speech*. These may make a number of forms, including:

- **rhyme:** words containing the same vowel sound, e.g. *Beanz Meanz Heinz*
- **rhythm:** words arranged in a regular pattern of stressed and unstressed syllables, e.g. *If you want to get ahead, get a hat*
- **repetition:** the use of the same word more than once; e.g. *No waste, no mess, no stress*
- **alliteration:** words beginning with, or containing, the same consonant sounds, e.g. *Big Beefy Bovril*
- **jingles, slogans or catch-phrases:** short phrases that sum up a message and are easy to remember, e.g. *American Express: That'll do nicely, sir.*

'Advertisements work. If they didn't, companies wouldn't spend so much money on them.'

Getting your point across

Persuasive language is not used just to sell products to consumers. It can have many purposes, including health and safety promotion, political

SECTION 2

IMPROVING YOUR SKILLS

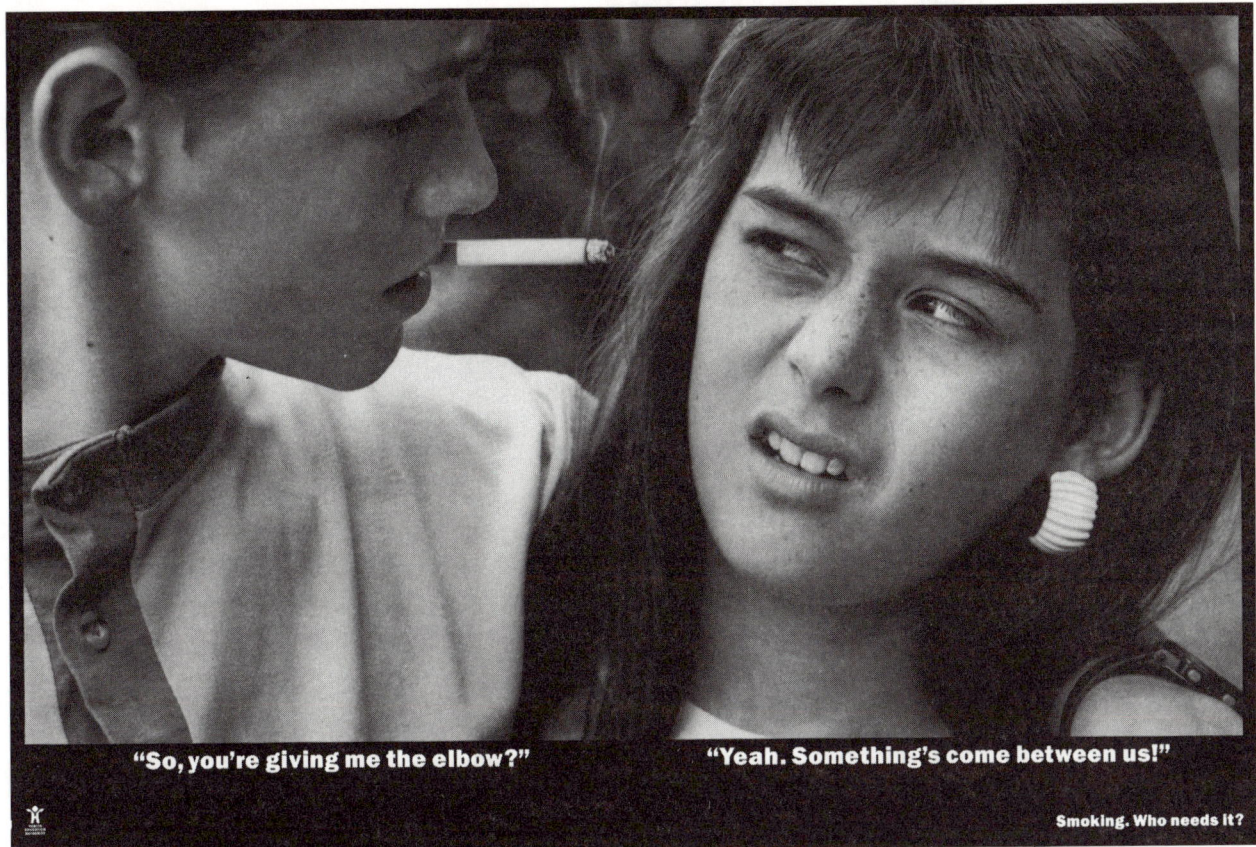

"So, you're giving me the elbow?" "Yeah. Something's come between us!"

Smoking. Who needs it?

and protest campaigning, and providing the public with information. Whenever we want to get a message across to a large number of people we use persuasive techniques.

Look at the poster above. It has been used by the Health Education Authority to try to persuade young people not to take up smoking. Before it was made, the designers had to decide:

- what effect they wanted to create, e.g. shock, disgust, humour
- what images they would use to create that effect
- what words they would use
- where they would place their poster, e.g. which magazines, what public places

Posters and pamphlets warning or protesting about a whole range of issues, from bloodsports to road-building, are becoming an increasingly common part of our society. As with advertising, it is important not just to look at what they mean on the surface. In this way you can avoid allowing yourself to be manipulated.

Have you got what it takes to write advertising copy? Try Exercises 4 and 5 on page 32 of Do It Yourself.

29

THE LANGUAGE OF PERSUASION
DO IT YOURSELF

Do It Yourself

Activities marked with a * have answers, or suggested answers, in the Answers section at the back of the book.

> To realise how you are being influenced, you need to recognise the difference between fact and opinion.

1 * Look at the following list of statements. Which are facts and which are opinions?
   (a) The world is round.
   (b) Men are superior to women.
   (c) Smoking can damage your health.
   (d) Capital punishment cuts crime.
   (e) Soccer was invented in England.
   (f) War is always wrong.
   (g) The English are the best at soccer.
   (h) The air is mostly made up of nitrogen.
   (i) Unemployment causes crime.
   (j) Germany is a part of Europe.

2 * Look carefully at the wording of the advertisement shown opposite, then answer the following questions:
   (a) What is uncertain about the meaning of the phrase 'the product that people prefer'?
   (b) What questions would you want to ask before you would be able to decide whether to be impressed by the claim about research findings?
   (c) What unusual features of language can you find in this advertisement?
   (d) What does the word 'unique' mean? What does the phrase 'unique formula' suggest? How could this claim be tested?
   (e) What would need to be true about the price for it to deserve the description 'bargain'?

3 * In each of the following pairs of words, which word has positive associations and which has negative associations?
   (a) shrewd   dishonest
   (b) inquiring   suspicious
   (c) showing off   displaying
   (d) confident   arrogant
   (e) deceit   tact
   (f) propaganda   information
   (g) regular   monotonous
   (h) waste   sacrifice

SECTION 2
DO IT YOURSELF

SHIFTY'S NIFTY STAIN REMOVER

The Product that People Prefer

Recent research has shown that 8 out of 10 people recommend our product

It conquers those stubborn stains that no other product can shift

JUST RUB IT IN AND SEE THE DIRT LIFT OUT

IT'S A MIRACLE OF MODERN TECHNOLOGY
developed from a **UNIQUE FORMULA** in our laboratories

HURRY while stocks last!

Take advantage of our
SPECIAL BARGAIN PRICE

THE LANGUAGE OF PERSUASION
DO IT YOURSELF

  (i) fussy   meticulous
  (j) childlike   childish

4 Suggest names for the following new products:

  (a) A car that will appeal to young people.
  (b) A breakfast cereal that might appeal to people who are concerned about the environment.
  (c) A chocolate bar that senior citizens might buy.
  (d) A portable computer to appeal to people who bring a lot of work home from the office.
  (e) A perfume for the family man.
  (f) A bank-account designed for children aged from ten to fifteen.

5 Design your own advertisement for your product with the following:

- a catch-phrase, slogan or jingle
- a few short phrases which point out the benefits of your product
- a description of the photograph or scene you would like to use

Try to ensure that your advertisement appeals to the target-group.

SECTION

Effective Communication

3

CONTENTS

Formal and informal groups

❖

A class discussion

❖

One-to-one

❖

Presenting a talk

Skills You Need

You are expected to:
- communicate effectively in formal and informal situations
- be confident in speaking and listening for a variety of purposes
- take different roles in a group discussion
- interact effectively with individuals on a one-to-one basis
- summarise and present information

Improving Your Skills

Every day we encounter different situations which require us to work with other people in a group. How well or how badly we deal with these situations will depend, to a very considerable extent, on how effectively we use language to communicate with other people.

Groups are formed for a variety of purposes. If people want to change something in society they may form a *pressure-group*, for example. A group like this tries to influence others, often those in government, in order to bring about the change they want to see.

There can also be groups whose purpose is to keep something exactly as it is. A *conservation group* might be formed, for example, to try to

EFFECTIVE COMMUNICATION
IMPROVING YOUR SKILLS

'Language is power. Make sure you are in possession of that power.'

keep an area of land or a building as it always has been. Alternatively, a group may be formed to run an event, such as a festival, or to give structure to social or leisure time, like the committee of a sports club.

We use groups in almost every part of our daily lives. In fact, the ability to work successfully in groups has been an important factor in the success of human beings as a species. As society grows more and more complex, the demands it places upon its members become more and more varied. It is often helpful to work in a group in order to meet these demands an effectively as possible.

Formal and informal groups

One of the factors crucial to dealing effectively with any situation is our assessment of the *level of formality* that it requires. This is a similar idea to the notion of language register, which is discussed in Section 1. We automatically try to suit our behaviour to the occasion. For example, you would behave quite differently:

- ◆ at your brother's or sister's wedding
- ◆ when giving evidence in a court of law
- ◆ when watching a video at home with friends

The first two occasions are more formal than the third, and people may well be wearing special clothes which show that formality. Each situation has its own level of formality and, as well as judging the correct register of language to use, we may have to decide on the correct way to proceed. In a court of law, for example, the rules are clearly laid down. The judge will have a title, such as *sir* or *my lord*; only one person will speak at a time; and there will be a set order in which people are allowed to speak.

If you are sitting around with your friends trying to decide which video to watch, you do not need a set of rules. It is perfectly all right for people to interrupt each other. Of course, in the end, one or other of you may have to take on the role of getting everyone to make up their mind.

If you are taking part in a more formal group discussion, however, you will almost certainly have to agree on the rules before you begin. People will need to take on specific roles and accept responsibility for some of the functions that a group needs to perform. There are a number of ways of doing this.

SECTION 3
IMPROVING YOUR SKILLS

Committees
One way of organising a formal group that is used all the time is known as the *committee*. A committee needs the following things: a purpose, meetings, officers, an agenda.

Purpose
A committee can be formed by any group or people, anywhere. It might be a committee formed by residents to campaign for traffic-calming in their street, for example.

Frequently a committee is formed as a smaller part of a larger organisation, like a group set up to run a sports tournament or a youth club. Many committees, such as a committee of members of parliament dealing with legislation, are given official and legal status.

Meetings
The discussions which the members of a committee have and any decisions that they make take place at *meetings*.

Officers
The officers have particular jobs to do. Permanent committees, which go on for meeting after meeting, normally elect their officers by voting for them. The officers are appointed for fixed periods of time, usually a year.

Chair
The person in charge is known as the *chairman*, *chairwoman* or sometimes just the *chair*. He or she has to take responsibility for opening and closing a meeting of the group, and is also the person who moves a meeting on from one stage to another.

Secretary
Someone needs to make notes about what is said. This person is known as the *secretary*. The notes are known as the *minutes* of the meeting. They are generally taken down in rough during the meeting and then written up carefully afterwards. Each meeting usually starts with everyone looking at the written-up minutes of the previous meeting, to make sure that they agree with what was recorded.

There are some opportunities to get involved in group discussion in Do It Yourself, Exercise 1 on page 43. Read the introductory paragraph first.

35

EFFECTIVE COMMUNICATION
IMPROVING YOUR SKILLS

Committees may also have other officers, for different purposes. For example, if the committee handles money, it will need a *treasurer*. If it has things it wants advertised or written about, it may have a *publicity officer*, and so on.

Agenda
The list of subjects or *items* which a committee considers in one meeting is called an *agenda*. In a good committee, everyone has an opportunity to choose an item which will be added to the list.

Reporting back
A committee may sometimes ask an individual member to go off and find out about something, or to do something. Then, afterwards, that member will report back to the larger group on what has been achieved.

Group size
Groups can be any size, but the larger they get, the harder they are to operate. Very often a large group can work best by splitting up into small groups to do certain things.

Decision making
A formal committee will always hold a vote on any matter about which it needs to take action. Most people are familiar with this process, though perhaps not all of it. There are five stages:
1. Someone *proposes* (puts forward) a suggestion.
2. The proposal is discussed.
3. The chair asks members to vote for or against the suggestion; no member may do both. Members are not obliged to vote, however – they can *abstain*.
4. The chair counts the votes on either side.
5. If there are more votes for the proposal than against, it is agreed, or *carried*.

Sometimes a member who disagrees strongly with a proposal, but is outvoted, will ask for his or her view to be put on record by being noted in the minutes.

Delegates
Sometimes a committee needs to report to a larger group. One or more members are chosen, usually by voting, to speak for the committee. This process is known as *delegating* and the person chosen is a *delegate*.

See if you could draw up an agenda for a meeting. You will have to think carefully about the scope of the task that the committee members have undertaken to carry out. See Exercise 2 of Do It Yourself on page 44.

SECTION 3
IMPROVING YOUR SKILLS

Informal groups
Not every group needs to be organised as formally as these. It is possible to work in groups which are less structured but still have rules of procedure.

One of the most basic functions of any small group is discussion. In order to know what people think about any situation, it is necessary to engage in discussion.

Listening
Listening to others is a skill that comes more easily to some of us than to others. Some people are always wanting to speak, and will completely dominate a group. For this reason, it is always a good idea to develop a system which allows people to take it in turns to speak.

Responding
There should be opportunities for people to respond to what others have said, or to add to earlier comments they made. It should not be difficult to agree to raise a hand to show readiness to speak.

Group leader
Even in an informal group, it usually helps to have a group leader. This can be rotated as frequently as group members decide is necessary. The leader can ensure that people speak in turn by choosing which of the people with their hands up is next.

Scribe
Even an informal group generally needs somebody to take notes. Sometimes known as the scribe, this person's role is very similar to that of a secretary. However, he or she is unlikely to be called on to write up the minutes of the meeting. As with other group-roles, it is a good idea to take the scribe's duties in rotation.

Consensus
Although all members of a group need to develop their skills in negotiation, this applies especially to the group leader, whose job it is to keep the group working smoothly and to help it reach agreement. Getting everyone's agreement, or even the agreement of a majority of group members, is quite an art. Getting this general agreement is known as achieving *consensus*.

'Remember to listen to everyone. People who are too anxious to talk often miss interesting points others have made.'

Now's your chance to observe group dynamics at first-hand. Try Exercise 2 on page 44.

37

EFFECTIVE COMMUNICATION
IMPROVING YOUR SKILLS

A class discussion

Group working is often used in schools as a way of learning. Working in a group with others helps in a number of ways, including:

- information pooling – finding out what others think
- brainstorming – coming up with ideas and hearing other people's suggestions
- problem solving – finding solutions.

The practical organisation of this can be difficult, however, and so it helps to organise the process. This is often the role of the teacher. Your teacher may ask your class to break up into groups to discuss a subject, for example. The topic, or *stimulus*, for the discussion may be chosen by the teacher or by the class.

Your teacher is likely to want the discussion to be held to a timetable, such as fifteen minutes to discuss ideas and another five minutes to agree conclusions. The teacher may ask you to choose whether you wish to take on roles within the group, such as group leader or scribe. He or she may also want you to meet with another group(s) at a given time, to share ideas. Sometimes you may be asked to move from group to group, to prevent one group from getting stale.

Finally, a delegate from each group may be asked to represent the views of that group to the whole class. This is known as holding a *plenary session*. The teacher will normally act as the chair of this plenary session and may summarise the views of each group.

KIND OF GROUP	ROLES	WAYS OF WORKING	DECISION MAKING
Formal			
Committee	Chair	Agenda	Voting
	Secretary	Minutes	
Informal			
Discussion	Group leader	Subject/Topic	Consensus
	Scribe	Notes	

SECTION 3

IMPROVING YOUR SKILLS

STIMULUS
Topic is introduced to class by teacher

↓

SCHEDULE
Class breaks up into smaller groups
Group members are given roles and timetable

↓

DISCUSSION
Ideas are introduced and considered
Opinions are offered
Notes are taken

↓

CONSULTATION
Meetings between individual groups may take place at intervals
Individual group members may move from group to group
Groups may keep separate

↓

CONCLUSIONS
Groups agree on their ideas or opinions
A delegate is chosen to speak for the group

↓

PLENARY SESSION
Groups return to class
Delegates express views and opinions of their groups
Teacher may summarise the findings of the class

EFFECTIVE COMMUNICATION
IMPROVING YOUR SKILLS

One-to-one

Working one-to-one with another person can be less difficult or more difficult than working in a group. There are fewer people to take into consideration, but the spotlight is on you all the time.

There are a number of ways in which you can interact with one other person using language, and, as with a group, these can have various levels of formality. One of the most formal ways is an *interview*.

An interview

An interview is a series of questions which one person puts and another answers. People use interviews in business and politics, journalism and entertainment, for finding employees, reporting situations, assessing the mood of the public, finding out more about a particular individual or event.

Setting up the interview

Before you begin an interview you should contact the interviewee (the person to be interviewed) and arrange a mutually convenient date and time. It is also important to set a time-limit for the interview, but be prepared to over-run if you need to and if your interviewee agrees.

Prepare a list of questions in advance. If you are not able to draw up a detailed set of questions, at least decide on the line of questioning you are going to use. This way you will avoid running out of things to say or finding yourself asking the same question twice using different words.

Try to frame your questions in such a way that you give the speaker a chance to explain what he or she thinks, rather than just giving one word answers. Questions that give the person interviewed scope to answer fully are known as *open questions*. The key words to start an open question are:

'Make your questions open-ended.'

| Who? | Why? | What? | When? | Where? | Which? | How? |

Any question beginning with one of these words cannot be answered with simply 'yes' or 'no'.

During the interview

Speak slowly and clearly and look at the speaker when you ask your questions. Always listen carefully to the answers given. Genuine listening will produce questions not on the list. So it is essential to be flexible and react to the information you receive.

The tone of your voice should show your warmth and appreciation, and using the person's name can also help to put your interviewee at ease, although you should not overdo this. What you are trying to do is to establish a *rapport* or relationship with your interviewee.

A questionnaire

Another way of finding out the views of other people is to draw up a *questionnaire*. A questionnaire is a written set of questions. These can be simple yes/no questions or they can be devised with a number of possible answers from which the person answering has to choose. Here is an example of how you develop questions for a questionnaire.

Imagine you wanted to find out what television programmes people at your school watched; you could just send everyone a sheet and write at the top: 'Which television programmes do you watch?' People do not always remember what they watch, however. It might be better to remind them by providing a list of programmes and asking whether they watched any of them.

If you wanted to find out which programmes were watched regularly, you could offer a number of alternative answers. For example, suppose that you wanted to find out how often people watched a programme called 'Neighbourhood' that was on five nights a week; you could put your question as shown above right.

You could use a questionnaire as part of your research for a written or spoken report on a subject.

Do you think you would make a good interviewer? Why not have a go? Try Exercise 3 on page 44 of Do It Yourself.

'Make eye contact, and be friendly and positive, but not demanding.'

How often do you watch 'Neighbourhood'?

Please tick the box that is nearest your actual viewing.

(a) I have never watched it. ☐
(b) I have watched it a few times. ☐
(c) I watch it about once a week. ☐
(d) I watch it more than once a week. ☐
(e) I watch every episode ☐

Practise the art of asking questions – make up your own questionnaire in Exercise 4 on page 44 of Do It Yourself.

EFFECTIVE COMMUNICATION
IMPROVING YOUR SKILLS

Presenting a talk

Making a presentation on a subject or giving a talk can be a very demanding task. There are a number of things you should remember.

Level of detail

It is important to judge the right amount of detail to go into. As with formality, there is a level appropriate to each situation. One way of helping you judge this properly is to try your report, or parts of it, by reading it aloud to a friend before you deliver it.

Being confident

It makes a big difference to what people think of your report if you give it in a relaxed manner. This gives the audience time to understand fully what you are saying. It also gives you time to think as you speak and to take in the audience's reaction.

It is essential to get to know your speech thoroughly beforehand. However, if your report is at all lengthy, do *not* try to learn the whole thing by heart. Even people who do this professionally, like presenters, cannot remember huge chunks. They would split it up into shorter pieces.

Structure your talk

Above all, you need to structure what you want to say. Whether you are speaking to one other individual, talking in a group or giving a speech at a formal occasion, you need to arrange what you say in manageable sections.

Write out the headings or thoughts, or the first sentence of each paragraph; this will remind you of what follows. To begin with, before you have learnt to give a talk well, you may find it helpful to write the speech out underneath these headings, but reading from notes is not as good as a spontaneous talk. The most important thing is to have thought about the subject really carefully and to try to relax and feel confident about saying what you think.

Using a spider diagram

Some people find it helpful to use a device such as a *spider diagram* to generate ideas and structure them. This allows you to show the connections between ideas in the most simple way possible. You start with one idea and then branch out in different directions as further ideas are suggested. The spider diagram shown opposite has been drawn by a pupil who plans to give a talk about water.

‘Your audience should affect what you say and how you say it.’

‘Write out the headings of each paragraph.’

The more practice you have in giving a talk, the greater will be your confidence. Try out on your friends some of the topics in Exercise 5 of Do It Yourself on page 45.

SECTION 3
DO IT YOURSELF

Mind map with **WATER** at the centre, branches to:
- hardness, softness
- canals
- water transport
- barges
- ships, shipping
- sea
- tides
- washing
- baptism
- weather
- crops, irrigation
- trace elements
- sewers
- drinking
- cooking
- sport and leisure
- lakes
- reservoirs
- fish, fishing
- rivers
- pollution
- waterfalls, hydroelectric power

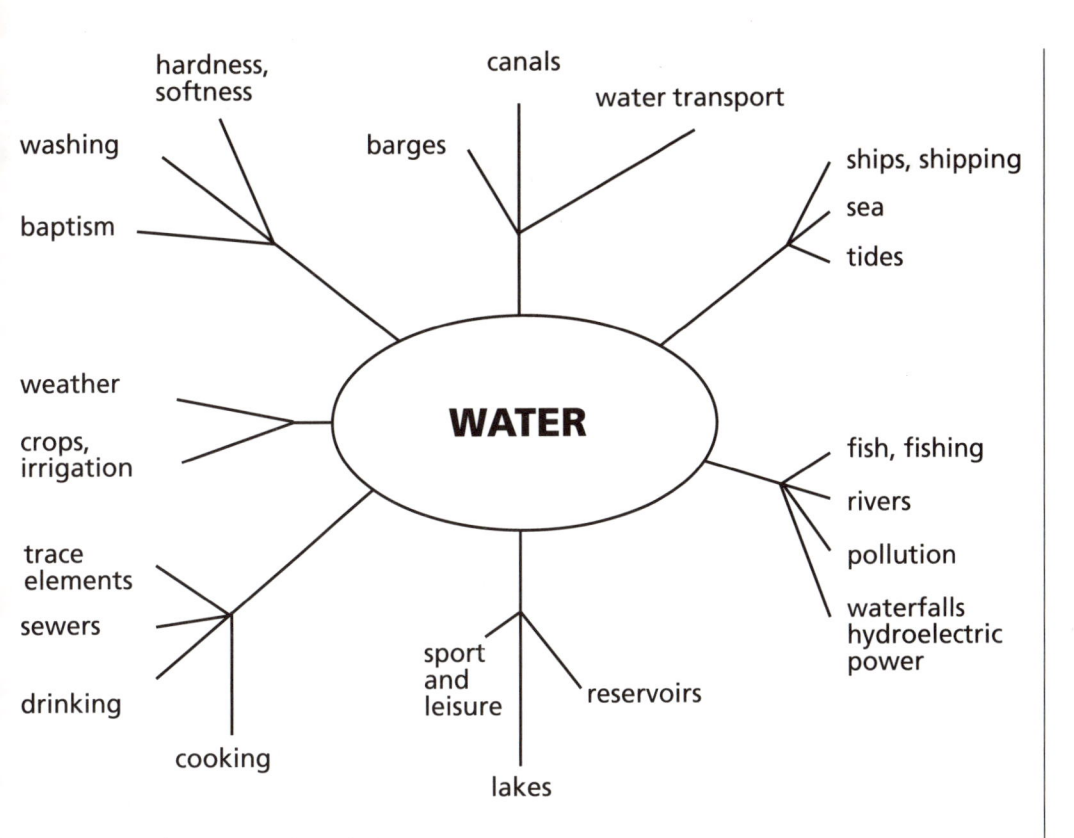

Do It Yourself

Activities marked with a * have answers, or suggested answers, in the Answers section at the back of the book.

Your group discussion (Exercise 2) would be helped by the presence of a neutral observer, or observers, who do not take part in the discussion but can give 'feedback' later on how it was conducted and what was achieved.

1 In groups, discuss one or more of the following topics for up to ten minutes each, with one group member taking the role of chair and another taking the role of secretary. Swap roles each time. Try to practise the skills you have learned. For example, as secretary, you should particularly concentrate on what is being said, and take notes briefly and quickly. As chair, you should start and finish discussions, and aim to achieve consensus. Here are some topics for discussion.

   (a) What is wrong with the present education system?
   (b) Does Britain need a monarchy?

EFFECTIVE COMMUNICATION
DO IT YOURSELF

(c) Is capital punishment necessary?
(d) What is the biggest threat to the modern world?
(e) What would you do about the ever-increasing traffic on our roads?
(f) What are the most important things in life?
(g) What rights do you think young people should have at the ages of:
(i) seven   (ii) thirteen

2* A meeting is one of the best ways of reaching agreement between people. However, meetings need to be planned. How many of these meetings could you plan? On your own, or in a group, choose one of the following meetings, then write out a list of items you might expect to see on an agenda for it.

(a) A meeting of pupils/students in your year at school, trying to plan a poster campaign to improve attitudes and behaviour in your school.
(b) A meeting of a committee formed to organise an end-of-year party in your school.
(c) A meeting of a group of young people who are going on a foreign student exchange holiday.
(d) A meeting of people of your own age who are trying to stage a play.
(e) A meeting of a group of musicians to draw up an advertisement for a new member.

You might find it helps to write the items on your agenda as a series of questions, such as:
(i) What are the problems?

> *'You need to have your questions prepared beforehand.'*

3 Carry out some interviews to be published in a school magazine. Ask people how well school prepares you for life. Talk to:
(a) someone of your own age who knows what he or she is doing after leaving school
(b) someone who has been at your school for less time than you
(c) a teacher
(d) someone roughly the same age as your parents

4 Devise a questionnaire that would enable you to find out the preferences of people of your own age. For each of the following categories, design questions that can be answered by ticking one answer out of a choice of two or three.
(a) music
(b) films
(c) hobbies
(d) television programmes

SECTION 3

DO IT YOURSELF

5 Prepare a talk to a group of people of your own age on one of the topics listed below. Before you begin you should think about the audience you are speaking to. Many people find it helps to imagine they are aiming the talk at one particular person they know.

A talk is best rehearsed but not over-rehearsed. It helps to tackle it in stages: first choose a topic, and write down your ideas. Now arrange them in order, then write notes on each one.

Your talk should not sound like you are reading it out. That is a lecture. When you give a talk you should try to be *spontaneous*, or natural. Strangely enough, as any actor will tell you, you need to practise in order to sound spontaneous. So practise your talk with notes and also without notes.

Use one of the following suggestions as the basis for your talk.
- **(a)** the commonest mistake parents make
- **(b)** a family holiday
- **(c)** junk food
- **(d)** the trouble with Christmas
- **(e)** an ideal school
- **(f)** fashion
- **(g)** why people find it so hard to live together
- **(h)** fox hunting
- **(i)** what I would do if I had one thousand pounds
- **(j)** where I live

Take it in turns to give a talk and to listen to each other's talks. Each member of the audience should prepare a question based on the talk. At the end of each one, the person giving the talk should be prepared to answer at least three questions about it. Remember, think of questions that need more than just a simple yes/no answer.

'Get to know your speech but don't learn it by heart.'

45

SECTION

4 | Researching and Reporting

CONTENTS

Researching

❖
Writing reports

❖
Writing narrative

❖
Reported speech

Skills You Need

You ought to be able to:
- assemble, summarise and use information from different sources
- select and use organisational devices, such as headings
- use the correct syntax and vocabulary for formal writing
- redraft work, paying attention to clarity, vocabulary, grammar and structure

Improving Your Skills

Our society grows every day. All over the world, all the time, millions of people are gathering data, processing it and producing information. A huge amount of this information is in English, because English is spoken by about 350 million people. Three-quarters of the world's mail is in English and five of the largest broadcasting companies of the world transmit in English. It is impossible to keep up with all of it!

SECTION 4

IMPROVING YOUR SKILLS

Researching

The human brain is an extraordinarily complex organ. It is very selective about the information it stores. It keeps enough skills, knowledge, memories and functions available to its user for the demands of existence. What it doesn't do, except for certain unusual individuals, is try to remember every single piece of information about everything.

Originally, of course, human beings did have to commit huge chunks of verbal knowledge to memory, such as which people were descended from which families. This was before there were written records.

Nowadays there is a huge variety of information sources available, which you can turn to whenever you need to look up some kind of information. These can be either formal or informal.

Formal information sources

A dictionary

The dictionary is the first information source most people are introduced to. They use a dictionary if they are not sure about the spelling of a word. At the top of each page of the dictionary, one word is given in bold type. This is known as the *headword*, and all the other words on the page will follow that in alphabetical order.

If you are not sure how a word begins, you may not be able to find it using a dictionary. You might be better trying a *spell-checker*. This is a computer program that forms part of most word processing packages and can also be bought separately.

A dictionary supplies a great deal of other information, as well as the spelling of the word. The main piece of information which it provides is a meaning, or range of meanings, for a word. If a word has more than one meaning, a dictionary usually puts the commonest, or most modern, first, like this:

forge 1 to write or paint like somebody else in order to deceive people
2 place where a blacksmith works

Dictionaries differ as to what other information they provide. They may tell you how to pronounce a word, especially if it is not in common use. This information is usually put in brackets, like this: *station (stay-shun)*.

Often dictionary writers use special symbols to indicate how letters should be pronounced, and these will be listed at the beginning of the book. A dictionary may also tell you what part of speech a word is, e.g. *station (n)*. The (n) is short for *noun*. (For an explanation of nouns and other parts of speech, turn to page 73.)

47

RESEARCHING AND REPORTING
IMPROVING YOUR SKILLS

A thesaurus

A thesaurus looks a bit like a dictionary but it is quite different. It makes use of *headwords*, but words are grouped according to associations (things they have in common). After each headword, there are groups of words or phrases which have something in common with that headword. At the back of the thesaurus all the headwords are listed in alphabetical order in an index, so that you can look them up and find out what page they are on. The index also contains *cross-references*, that is, the numbers of other headwords in which the same subject appears.

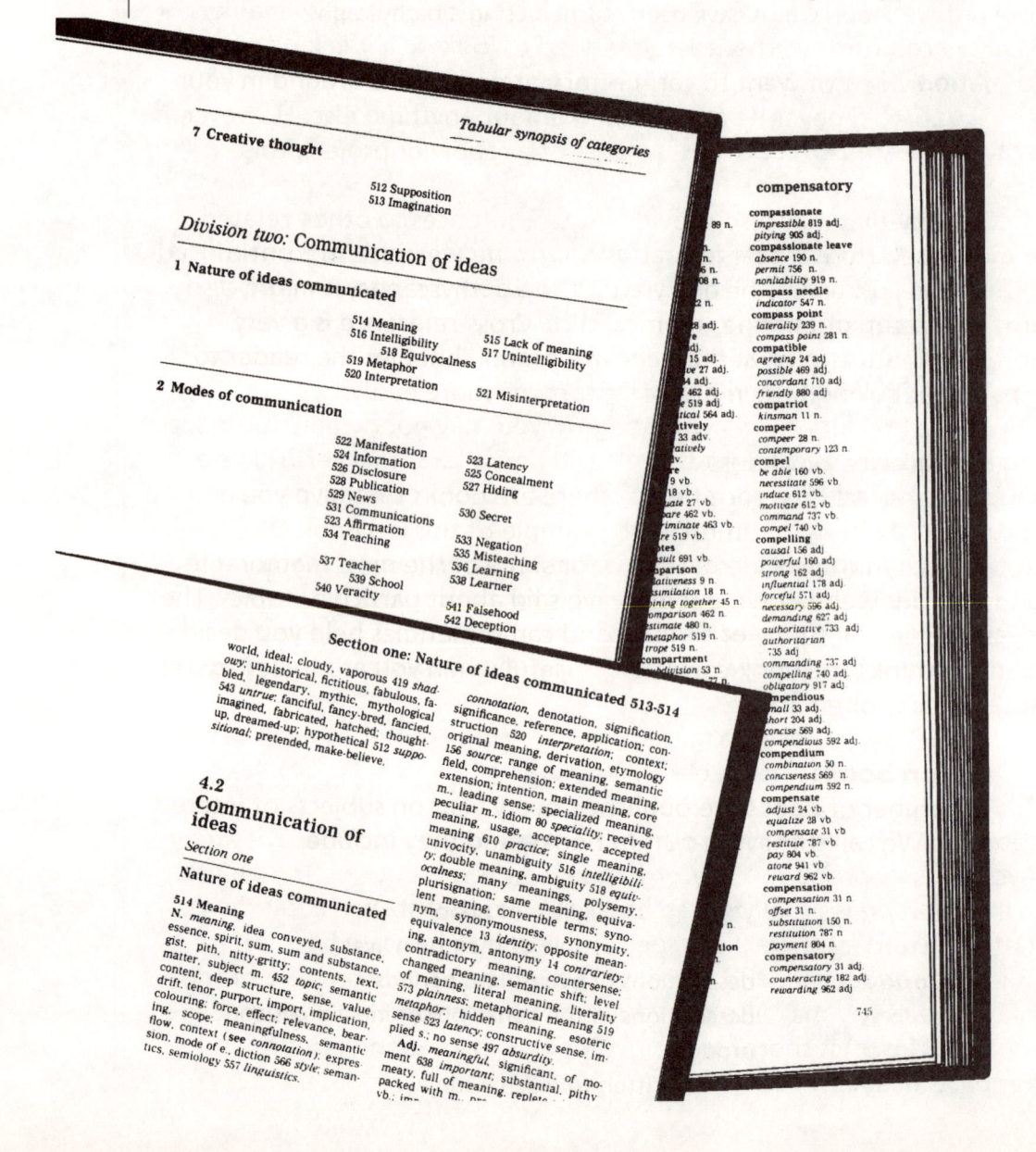

An encyclopaedia

Encyclopaedias are arranged, like dictionaries, in alphabetical order. They too make use of headwords. However, they contain much more detailed information about their entries. For example, if you looked up the word 'bathyscaphe' in even quite a basic encyclopaedia, you would learn:

- that it was an underwater vessel for exploring the ocean depths
- the name and date of the first bathyscaphe
- the name of the inventor of the first bathyscaphe
- the depths which have been reached using a bathyscaphe

You certainly do not want to carry information like this around in your head; you would never be able to think about anything else. However, if you were writing about the sea as part of a report or project, this information might be useful.

Encyclopaedias may also provide cross-references to other, related topics. These often appear in brackets with the word *see* in front of them. If you looked up the entry about the bathyscaphe, it might also say: (*see*: ocean, submarine, submersible). Cross-reference is a very important feature in presenting information. It enables the reader to move about through the maze of facts much more easily.

Other reference books

As well as general reference books, there are books that give you a particular kind of information. One example of this is a Book Of Quotations, which provides a source for some of the most memorable things various well-known people have said about particular topics. The quotations can be funny or serious, and can sometimes help you decide what you think. The book can also be useful when you are trying to write an essay or an article.

Non-fiction books

A huge number of books are published every year on subjects of interest to people. We call these *non-fiction* books, and they include:

manuals	for cars, computers etc.
biographies	accounts of the lives of people
autobiographies	accounts by people of their own lives
histories	descriptions of events and periods
sociology	descriptions of the behaviour of individuals and groups
textbooks	books written to teach a subject

RESEARCHING AND REPORTING
IMPROVING YOUR SKILLS

Scanning texts
Using reference books would be very laborious if you had to read through every one to find the information you were looking for, so it is important to develop your *scanning* and *skimming* skills.

Scanning means quickly running your eye down the page of a book looking for what you want, without necessarily taking everything in. We often do this when we use the Index or Contents of a book, or a telephone directory.

We skim when we read fast. We look for the main points and 'clues' connected with the subject we are researching. These clues are often found in section headings, keywords, the opening and closing sentences of paragraphs and chapters, summaries and conclusions. Skimming is useful for selecting the information for brief notes and for collecting page references.

'Skim and scan when reading for information.'

Collating information
Putting all the information from different sources together so that it makes sense is known as *collating*. Usually this involves you writing everything out again after having selected the information, organised it and considered the audience and purpose.

It can also be extremely helpful to have a *paste-up* session first. This means assembling the work in rough, temporarily sticking in any illustrations, and cutting and pasting pieces of text for which you want to change the order.

Cutting and pasting text is much easier if you have been able to write it on a computer. Using photocopies can also be a helpful strategy when you are creating a paste-up.

'Raw material needs organising.'

Informal information sources
There are other ways of finding information. People who write biographies, autobiographies or histories will have to look at *informal sources* as well as formal ones, such as census returns, newspapers, oral evidence, photographs, letters and diaries.

50

Oral evidence

This simply means conversations or interviews. If, for example, you wanted to know your great-grandmother's date of birth, the obvious thing to do would be to ask your father or mother. If you cannot, or they do not know, you may have to go to the official place where family records are kept (in England this is St Catherine's House).

Oral questions like this can be a first line of research, when you have access to people who are involved in any way. This is important when you are researching something that has just happened or something that is fairly recent history, for example within the last seventy-five years.

Photographs

Photographs can help people remember events or people. They remind us of what has happened and of what things were like at the time the photograph was taken.

Letters and diaries

Letters are not written as often as they used to be. The invention of the telephone, the fax and electronic mail has seen to that. However, people still write personal letters, particularly when they are living in separate countries.

A diary is rather like one long letter which you keep writing to yourself. Many people imagine that keeping a diary means writing every day. Some people do this, of course, but others simply keep a record of thoughts or of things that happened to them on a particular day. Sometimes extraordinary things happen to us – we go on a holiday with friends; we meet someone we really like; we achieve something we have been struggling for, like passing a test or winning a competition. It is sometimes nice to look back on the way we felt at the time. Diaries can help us do this.

Other people's diaries and letters can also give us an idea of what their lives were like, how they thought and what they did.

There is a subject for research which will put your skills to the test. It is also a source of endless fascination to many people. You'll find it on page 59 of Do It Yourself, Exercise 1.

Writing reports

A report is an objective account of something. It is often the result of research or some sort of investigation.

Taking notes

Whatever sources you use to find out information, you will generally find it helpful to take notes. This is often a very personal thing, as you

RESEARCHING AND REPORTING
IMPROVING YOUR SKILLS

will know if you have ever tried to read anybody else's notes. As long as the notes are only for your own use, any system that works for you will do. If they are for others to read, however, then you need to make them clear. Here are some ways in which you can write things down quickly. Once you start note-taking, and thinking about how to do it as efficiently as possible, you will come up with your own shortcuts to use along with these.

- Use some symbols for words.
  t for *the*, *&* for *and* etc.
- Abbreviate words.
  dnsr for *dinosaur*
- Omit words.
  War started 1914 for *the war started in 1914*
- Use dashes instead of other punctuation.
  Beatles – pop group 60s – from Liverpool – first record 1963
- Use numbered points.
  1 Nicholas Copernicus
  2 1473–1543
  3 Polish scientist
  4 called 'Father of Astronomy'

Structuring your report
Whatever the subject of your report and whomever it is aimed at, it needs a clear structure so that listeners can follow with no difficulty. You should make use of markers and structural or organisational devices, such as a logical sequence of ideas, paragraphs, headings and subheadings, and examples or illustrations.

A logical sequence of ideas
One idea should follow another and they should all be leading somewhere. You might start with a *hypothesis* (a theory or idea), which you explain and then explore. You consider whether it is true or not, what it would mean if it were, how it would affect other things. This might also be described as developing a *theory* or *theme*.

Exploring a hypothesis like this means breaking it down into smaller parts and analysing it. This generally involves looking at the arguments for and against its being true and weighing them up.

You will find that some ideas are more important to your hypothesis or theme than others. Sorting out the ideas or arguments in order of importance is known as *prioritising*.

‘Good reports present ideas in a logical and orderly sequence.’

SECTION 4
IMPROVING YOUR SKILLS

Paragraphing

A whole page of writing that has not been set out in paragraphs is very difficult to read. Therefore every piece of writing above a certain length should be written in paragraphs. There are exceptions to this rule, of course. James Joyce, a very famous Irish author, wrote the entire last chapter of his book, *Ulysses*, in one paragraph! However, this was a special case. He was trying to describe the thoughts of someone passing into sleep. If you try to emulate him, you run the risk of your audience falling asleep.

If you have *prioritised* your ideas and your arguments properly, your writing should fall neatly into sections, or paragraphs. It is always a good idea to to look at these after a first draft, to see if it might not be better to put the breaks in different places.

Headings and subheadings

It helps to give different sections headings and even subheadings. These should be short – just a few lines saying what the section will be about. Newspapers and magazines use this method all the time because it makes the writing easier to take in.

Examples or illustrations

Giving examples of what you mean helps people to understand you. If someone says that they like *modern music*, they might mean a whole range of different kinds of music. You would need to ask them to give you an example of the sort of thing they like, if you were thinking of buying them a record as a present!

Examples give people extra information. They help to pin down an idea or a description. Photographs, charts, coloured illustrations, diagrams can all have the same effect as examples when they are used in the right way, in the right place.

Getting the tone right

Sometimes we need to invert or change round the order of a sentence, especially when we want to sound more formal or impersonal: 'Viewers complain about television programmes' becomes 'Complaints have been made by viewers about certain television programmes'. You often hear this inverted tone adopted on news programmes, since it makes the news items sound more objective or unbiased.

We also use an impersonal tone for writing up experiments or investigations in school subjects such as Science, History, Geography, Maths and Technology.

'Make full use of ways of presenting data.'

'Before you begin to write, decide what type of writing it will be.'

The writing process
Whatever your subject and audience, writing a report is something that has to be done in stages.

Stage 0 Pre-writing
Before you begin to write, decide what type of writing you want to produce, in what style and for what purpose or audience.

Stage 1 Planning
Look back at the notes you have made. Prioritise your ideas and arguments. Organise them into paragraphs. Think about how you are going to begin and how you hope to end. Since this is a report, you may be making recommendations, so work out what they will be.

Stage 2 A first draft
Write up your report, following the sequence you have decided on. Afterwards, check it through to see if anything has been left out. Read each other's work if you are taking part in a group project.

Stage 3 Criticising your draft
This involves thinking like a reader and looking at the content. Does it say what you want it to say? Does it say it in the most effective way, or can you improve the way you have put things? Look again at your recommendations. Are they manageable, sensible and possible?

Stage 4 A final draft
Writing your final draft requires you to exercise all your presentational skills. Check the spellings of all the words you are unsure about. Use either a dictionary or a spell-checker. Think about the punctuation. Have you written any long sentences which could be broken up by using commas, or even made into a number of shorter sentences?

Your final draft should be well presented with appropriate sections and headings. You can make this clearer by numbering or giving a letter to individual sections or items. Do not forget to make use of examples and illustrations where these would improve the clarity of your writing.

Now you are ready to sign and date your report.

Handwriting causes problems for a lot of people. Some of the most brilliant writers, thinkers or inventors have had appalling handwriting. Nevertheless, presentation is important. So, if you know that your handwriting could be better, try to do something about it. Here are a number of strategies you might adopt:

‘Your work needs to be well presented.’

SECTION 4
IMPROVING YOUR SKILLS

- take your time
- use a different pen
- hold your pen differently
- sit further away from your work
- deliberately change the slope of your writing

If you have access to a computer for word processing, take advantage of it and you will be pleased with the professionalism of the finished product.

Writing narrative

Narrative means story-telling. To write narrative well you need to learn to:
- devise a plot
- describe the setting
- create and describe characters

Plot
The plot is the basic story behind any piece of writing. Devising a plot means thinking before you start to write. Everyone has their own way of coming up with stories. It often helps to think of other stories you have read. Many writers like to be quite clear about what is going to happen in the story and how it will end, before they start to write. This way they avoid getting stuck halfway. You can do this by:
- making a plan of the main points of the story using numbered points
- writing out a short summary of your plot before you start
- telling your plot to a friend

Others prefer to leave a little bit of the plot unknown. They find that this makes the writing come alive. Either way, you should try to enjoy telling the story. Avoid rushing it. The more you become interested in your own story as you write, the more your audience will enjoy reading it.

Setting
Think about the books that you have most enjoyed reading, and why you enjoyed them. Often it is because they create a whole world which draws the reader in. This is the effect that every writer is seeking to achieve. The setting for your story can be one way of doing this. Try to visualise what is happening and find words to describe it. Too much description can hold up the plot, of course, but if there is not enough, the reader will find it hard to enter into the imaginary world of your story.

'Take advantage of a word processor if you have access to one.'

If you did Exercise 1, you might like to complete the job. If you do try Exercise 2 (page 59), then don't forget that your audience should affect what you say and how you say it.

55

RESEARCHING AND REPORTING
IMPROVING YOUR SKILLS

Characters
Above all, the reader needs to believe in the characters in your story. We can learn about the characters from what they say and do and what the writer tells us about them. To make your characters convincing, you need to believe in them yourself. You need to think hard about them, to imagine what their lives are like, and how they feel about things, especially how they feel about what is happening in the story and about the other characters.

Writers often base their characters on people they know or have met. This does not mean that everything about a character in a book will be the same as the person it is based on. The author may just choose a few details he or she has observed, such as a way of speaking or behaving, or details of someone's physical appearance. Most characters in books are, in fact, mixtures of all the people that the writer has ever come across.

A title can make a good starting point for writing a story. Turn to page 60 to see if any of the ideas in Do It Yourself Exercise 4 inspires you.

Reported speech

When you write down what people have said, there are three main ways to organise your writing. These are known as direct speech, indirect speech and scripted speech.

Direct speech
Direct speech means using the exact words someone said and putting speech marks (also known as quotation marks or inverted commas) round them to show it. Direct speech is used when writing a story or when quoting someone's words. These are the basic rules for setting out direct speech:

- ◆ The words which are spoken should go in between speech marks, e.g. 'Come here at once!', and should begin with a capital letter.
- ◆ The words which tell us who spoke, e.g. *he said, she replied*, etc., should not be included between the speech marks.
- ◆ A comma is used to separate these two sets of words, e.g. I said, 'Who are you?'
- ◆ You should show when a new speaker has spoken by starting a new paragraph.

If you are quoting from someone's speech or statement, the quote is likely to go on for more than one paragraph. In this case, you should put speech marks at the beginning of each new paragraph, but you do not need to close them at the end of the paragraph. Close the speech marks only at the very end of the statement or speech.

Indirect speech

Indirect speech means using your own words to express what someone else said. These are the basic rules for setting out indirect speech:

- The first person singular (I) is changed to the third person singular (he/she)

    direct speech   John said, '**I** think it is raining.'
    indirect speech   John said that **he** thought it was raining.

- The word 'that' is sometimes added, as in the above example, although it can be left out.

    indirect speech   He said that he thought it was raining
    or   He said he thought it was raining.

- The tense of the verb is changed. Present tense becomes past tense, and a verb that is already in the past tense is put even further into the past. 'Will' (future tense) becomes 'would' (conditional tense).

    direct speech   Elizabeth said, 'I *am* going home.'
    indirect speech   Elizabeth said she *was* going home.
    direct speech   Stephen said, 'I *have* finished my meal.'
    indirect speech   Stephen said that he *had* finished his meal.
    direct speech   The policeman said, 'I *will* go there as soon as possible.'
    indirect speech   The policeman said that he *would* go there as soon as possible.

- Quotation marks are omitted.

    direct speech   Ali said, 'I am going to the party at 8.00.'
    indirect speech   Ali said that he was going to the party at 8.00.

Scripts

Dialogue can also be written out as a script. This is how an interview is written out. The name of the person speaking is written on one side and what he or she says on the other, like this.

    Interviewer: Have you been writing songs for a long time?
    Interviewee: It depends what you mean by a long time.

In an interview like this the names of both people may or may not be written. Sometimes the letters Q and A are used for the words *question* and *answer*.

A script format like this is also used for plays. The names of the characters are written first, followed by the words that they say. Although you can add some directions, they should be used sparingly. A

Now try your hand at reporting someone else's words. Exercise 3 on page 60 of Do It Yourself will give you something to practise on.

RESEARCHING AND REPORTING
IMPROVING YOUR SKILLS

good play traditionally concentrates on what is said and leaves the majority of the setting to the director.

Modern film or television scripts, however, may contain a continuous description of the action running parallel with the words. Scripts like this are usually produced by professionals.

The spoken word

Whichever way you choose to change speech into writing, you will notice ways in which they are different. When you speak, you can see from their body language if the person to whom you are speaking understands what you say. You can tell, also, if things are going wrong. However, when your write, you have to be much more careful.

Hesitation In speech there are hesitations, because we make things up as we go along and we need time to think and pause for a moment. Sometimes we fill in the 'thinking time' with 'and' or similar words.

Verbal props We also put in 'ums' and 'ers' to indicate that we have something else to say in a moment. Or we may start in a particular way and find out that what we have to say could be better put another way round, so we correct ourselves as we go along. We often use phrases like 'you know what I mean' or 'you see'. Such expressions are known as *verbal props*.

SECTION 4

DO IT YOURSELF

Do It Yourself

Activities marked with a * have answers, or suggested answers, in the Answers section at the back of the book.

For the activities in this section, there are no right or wrong answers. Try to find someone who is prepared to read and discuss your work with you – someone who will criticise constructively and help you to improve the skills which this section has set out to practise. Before you start, look again at Skills You Need.

1 Create your own Family Archive. This means finding out where your family came from, what the names and dates of birth and death of family members were, where they lived and who they married. Draw up your own Family Tree and discover as much background information as you can.
- Use formal information sources, such as birth, death and marriage certificates and parish registers.
- An important source is the public library, which holds the district's archive collection and census returns.
- Find out what you can from informal sources: talk to your relatives; ask them if you can rummage through old photographs, or whether there are any family letters or diaries that they would be prepared to let you read.
- Make notes on all the information you have gathered.
- Organise your notes carefully, to make the most of your material. You could create a filing system by using a separate card for each person and setting the details down under a series of headings.

Remember: You cannot write down everything. Be selective. Pick out the important facts. To save recording things more than once, use cross-references.

2 Use the information you have compiled for your Family Archive in Exercise 1 to write a report on your family. Structure it carefully. Either start with the present and work back through the generations, or vice versa. When the report is finished, show it to your family. Tracing a family's history is hard work, so they should be impressed. You should have a lot of fun, as well as learning a great deal about your roots.

59

RESEARCHING AND REPORTING

DO IT YOURSELF

3 * Read what Ron Stafford, the Chairman of Drakeham United Football Club, had to say at a press conference.

Thanks to everyone for turning up at such short notice. I've called this press conference for one reason and one reason alone. I want the public to know what's been going on at this club. But I want to emphasise right from the start that it's all been happening behind my back. As soon as I found out about it, I called you lot in, because I want people to know that my hands are clean. Have you got that?

Okay. Now, last week I overheard two of my players talking in the locker rooms after the match. They didn't know I was listening or they wouldn't have said what they did say. So what did they say? I'll tell you. They talked about the match being fixed. They talked about the goalkeeper being paid three thousand pounds to let that shot into the net. They talked about smaller payments to other players. And I got the impression that this has been going on for some time.

When they had gone, I immediately called an emergency meeting of the other directors. We interviewed the manager and all the players. The manager, goalkeeper and three others players have been suspended pending further enquiries. That is all I have to say for now. Thank you.

Write an article for the sports pages of a newspaper, explaining what has happened at Drakeham United. Use indirect speech to describe what Ron Stafford told the press, but do not try to include everything he said.

4 Write a story using one of the following as a title or starting point:
The Hardest Thing
Very Special Shoes
The Price You Pay
No Time like the Present
The Manager
Starstruck
Waiting for the Post
The Lesser of Two Evils
A Secret Life
Curiosity

SECTION

Using a Library

5

Skills You Need

You need to be able to:
- read a wide variety of literature and other texts
- read independently with responsiveness and enthusiasm
- be familiar with our literary heritage
- retrieve, handle and synthesise information.

Improving Your Skills

Ask most people what a library is for and they will answer: borrowing books. This is true, but there is much more to it than that. A library is a way of accessing the world of writing, just as a bank is a way of accessing the financial world.

How a library works

So much has been written on non-fiction subjects. So many stories have been written. The words of speeches and songs and poems, the knowledge and learning that our civilisation has built up over thousands of years have all been recorded in writing.

CONTENTS

How a library works

❖

Choosing books

❖

Creating a reading programme

USING A LIBRARY
IMPROVING YOUR SKILLS

> *Knowing how to get information for yourself is the first step towards having your own ideas.*

This is a lot of learning. The most learned professor at a university hopes only ever to know a tiny amount of all that there is to know. People who appear on quiz shows and answer detailed questions about their subjects or about general knowledge are still only dabbling a toe in the vast ocean of knowledge that makes up the world of learning. You can have access to that world through your library.

How books are arranged

People often want to read about their hobbies, interests or leisure pursuits, such as sport, gardening, food and drink, travel and the environment. They also enjoy reading about the lives of others and the times they have lived through. Sometimes books focus on famous people and the extraordinary events of their lives, like the assassination of President Kennedy or the campaigns of Gandhi and Martin Luther King. Books like this are all *non-fiction* and in a library they are classified according to the *Dewey Decimal System*.

The Dewey Decimal System

An American, Melvil Dewey (1851–1931), divided all knowledge into ten *classes* and gave each class a number, as follows:

- 000 general reference
- 100 philosophy, psychology
- 200 religion
- 300 social science
- 400 languages
- 500 pure science
- 600 applied science, technology
- 700 arts, crafts, recreation
- 800 literature
- 900 geography, biography, history

Have you got classification sorted out now? Then have a go at Exercise 1 of Do It Yourself on page 69.

Each shelf or set of shelves in a library is numbered according to this system and books are given a number as well, according to which of the ten classes they fall into. This process is called *classification*. The classification number is written on the spine. Subjects are sub-divided so that a book about playing the piano might have the number 786 within a library, the first number standing for the arts, the second for music, the third for the piano.

Classification by author

Non-fiction When you have used the Dewey system to find the shelf which has the subject you want, you will find the books arranged in alphabetical order, by the author's surname.

Fiction Fiction comes in a wide variety of genres (forms), such as:

- spy stories
- detective stories
- historical stories
- science fiction
- horror stories
- romance

Sometimes libraries will have whole shelves devoted to a particular genre. In general, however, all fiction is arranged on its own, in alphabetical order, and separate from the books with Dewey classification.

Authors with two surnames Sometimes people are uncertain where to look for authors whose last names are made up of more than one word. These are usually arranged according to the letter of the first word of the name.

Sir Arthur Conan Doyle can be found under 'C'.

The same rule applies to authors whose names contain apostrophes.

Sean O'Casey can be found under 'O'.

Choosing books

Consulting a catalogue

All libraries have catalogues which list the books that they have available. These catalogues may be in the form of a card index, with the details of each book on a separate card, or they may be printed on microfiche.

You can consult the catalogue to find out whether the library has:
- ◆ books about a certain subject in which you are interested
- ◆ books by a certain author
- ◆ a particular book

Many libraries also provide written book lists of what they have on popular subjects or by well-known authors.

See if you would know where to look for your favourite fiction authors – try Exercise 2 on page 69 of Do It Yourself.

❛Catalogues will help you to find the book you want.❜

USING A LIBRARY
IMPROVING YOUR SKILLS

Scanning books

As you get better able to read, you develop an ability to sample text. You look at the first few words, perhaps think about the first sentence, almost as if you are tasting the book. Then, if you like what you find, your mind begins skipping along the line, predicting what you will read next.

Reserving books

If you are unable to get a particular book in your school library, go to a public library. If they do not have a copy of the book, you may be able to reserve it. This involves filling out a form, giving the name of the author, the title of the book and any other details you have about it. The librarian will then consult the catalogue and see if it can be located. It is possible that the library does have the book but that someone else is currently borrowing it. In this case, your form will be kept until the book is returned. It will then be issued to you.

It is also possible that the book is in the library's *reserve stock*. Many libraries keep a proportion of their books, especially those which are less often requested, out of public display, that is, in stock.

Finally, if the librarian is unable to get a copy of the book from within the library's own stock, they will arrange to borrow the book for you from another library. So do not be afraid to ask the library staff for help.

Book details

Any enquiry about a particular book you are trying to find will be much easier to sort out if you can give the library staff as much information about it as possible. As well as the name of the author and the title of the book, they will want to know:

> **The publisher** This is the firm who pays for the book to be printed and bound, e.g. Ebury Press.
>
> **The publication date** You can usually find this on the back of the title page. It helps to know if a book is up-to-date or not. Opinions are always changing on subjects, as new methods are used or discoveries are made. This does not mean, however, that the older a book, the more likely it is to be wrong. Every book represents what people thought at the time and researchers, in particular, use publication dates to trace the way that opinion on a subject changes.
>
> **ISBN** This is the number which the publisher gives the book. ISBN stands for International Standard Book Number. Every book in the world has its own ISBN, and each one is different.

SECTION 5

IMPROVING YOUR SKILLS

Using books
A book can be a little like a library. You may need help finding your way around it. To make this easier, books are generally divided up into sections.

Contents The contents list is normally found at the front of the book, and provides a guide to the information in the book by listing chapter titles and the pages they start on.

Chapters These are the principal sections of a book. Both fiction and non-fiction books use chapters, and each chapter usually has its own number and title.

Index The index is generally found at the back of the book and is an alphabetical list of subjects covered in the book, with page numbers showing where the subject was mentioned. Any item in the index may have a number of page references if it appears more than once.

Creating a reading programme

Reading novels and short stories is an important part of everyone's education for many reasons, including the following:

- They are enjoyable.
- They broaden our experience.
- They help us understand human nature.
- They teach us things we did not know.

Creating your own Reading Programme makes this easier.

What books to include
It is important to read some pre-twentieth century works as well as modern ones. They are the stuff our literary heritage is made of. You should choose your own books, but here are some guidelines to help you decide.

Include at least one of each of the following:

- books you think you will like
- books you think you will not like
- books suggested by a friend
- books recommended by a teacher
- books everyone has heard the name of
- books you have heard the name of that sound attractive

On the following pages there are some suggestions to help you.

How well do you understand something you read? Find out in Do It Yourself, Exercises 3 and 4 on pages 69–72.

USING A LIBRARY
IMPROVING YOUR SKILLS

How to organise your programme
Give yourself targets and a timescale. Both of these need to be realistic. A book a fortnight might suit some people, while for others it might be too much or too little. You know how quickly you read. Do try to push your limit a bit.

Keep records
Record the names of the books you read, their authors and any feelings you had about them. Every so often, look back over your list and remember something from one of the books you have read.

Recommending reading
Pre-twentieth century literature
You may find some of these difficult to read, but it is worth persevering.

Author	Title
Louisa M Alcott	Little Women
Jane Austen	Pride and Prejudice
Charlotte Brontë	Jane Eyre
Daniel Defoe	Robinson Crusoe
Charles Dickens	Great Expectations
	David Copperfield
Thomas Hardy	Wessex Tales
Robert Louis Stevenson	Treasure Island
	Kidnapped
Mark Twain	Tom Sawyer
	Adventures of Huckleberry Finn

Twentieth century literature
These are books which are highly thought of and seem likely to become classics.

Anne Frank	The Diary Of Anne Frank
William Golding	Lord of the Flies
Grahame Greene	The Third Man
	Brighton Rock
Harper Lee	To Kill A Mockingbird
Laurie Lee	Cider With Rosie
George Orwell	Nineteen Eighty-four
	Animal Farm
John Steinbeck	The Pearl
	Of Mice and Men
J R R Tolkien	The Lord of the Rings

SECTION 5

IMPROVING YOUR SKILLS

Keith Waterhouse	Billy Liar
H G Wells	The Time Machine
	The War of the World

Modern children's fiction

The following titles vary widely in their levels of difficulty. You may enjoy some and dislike others. There is only one real way to find out.

Richard Adams	Watership Down
Joan Aiken	The Wolves of Willoughby Chase
Vivien Alcock	The Trial of Anna Cotman
Bernard Ashley	Terry on the Fence
	Running Scared
Stan Barstow	Joby
Nina Bawden	Carrie's War
	Kept in the Dark
Judy Blume	It's Not the End of the World
	Tiger Eyes
Ray Bradbury	The Golden Apples of the Sun
	October Country
Betsy Byars	The Nineteenth Emergency
	The Cartoonist
Peter Carter	Under Goliath
	Bury the Dead
Maude Casey	Over the Water
John Christopher	The Guardians
Beverley Cleary	Fifteen
Robert Cormier	The Chocolate War
	After the First Death
Helen Cresswell	Moondial
	The Secret World of Polly Flint
Gillian Cross	The Dark Behind the Curtain
	Wolf
Marjorie Darke	A Question of Courage
Anita Desai	The Village by the Sea
Peter Dickinson	The Weathermonger
	The Gift
Berlie Doherty	Granny Was a Buffer Girl
Anne Fine	Goggle Eyes
	A Pack of Liars
Pauline Fisk	Telling the Sea
Leon Garfield	Smith

67

USING A LIBRARY
IMPROVING YOUR SKILLS

Alan Garner	The Weirdstone of Brisingamen
	The Moon of Gomrath
Rosa Guy	The Friends
Nigel Hinton	Buddy
Anne Holm	I Am David
Jani Howker	Badger on the Barge
Toeckey Jones	Go Well, Stay Well
Brian Keaney	If This Is the Real World
	Boys Don't Write Love Stories
Robert Leeson	It's My Life
Ursual LeGuin	The Wizard of Earthsea
C S Lewis	The Magician's Nephew
	The Lion, the Witch and the Wardrobe
Joan Lingard	Across the Barricades
Penelope Lively	The Ghost of Thomas Kempe
	The Revenge of Samuel Stokes
Geraldine MacCaughrean	A Little Lower than the Angels
Michelle Magorian	Goodnight Mister Tom
Margaret Mahy	The Catalogue of the Universe
	The Haunting
Jan Mark	Thunder and Lightnings
Michael Morpurgo	The War of Jenkins' Ear
Beverly Naidoo	Journey to Jo'burg
	Chain of Fire
Robert O'Brien	Z for Zachariah
	Mrs Frisby and the Rats of NIMH
Katherine Paterson	Bridge to Terabithia
Jill Paton Walsh	Grace
Philipa Pearce	Tom's Midnight Garden
	The Way to Satin Shore
K M Peyton	Flambards
	A Midsummer Night's Death
Ann Pilling	Henry's Leg
Philip Pullman	The Broken Bridge
Ian Serraillier	The Silver Sword
Rosemary Sutcliff	The Eagle of the Ninth
	Dawn Wind
Mildred Taylor	Roll of Thunder Hear My Cry
J R R Tolkien	The Hobbit
John Townsend	Noah's Castle
	The Intruders

SECTION 5
DO IT YOURSELF

Cynthia Voigt	Tell Me if the Lovers Are Losers
	Homecoming
Robert Westall	The Machine Gunners
	The Scarecrows
Paul Zindel	The Pig Man

Do It Yourself

Activities marked with a * have answers, or suggested answers, in the Answers section at the back of the book.

1* Using the Dewey Decimal System shown here, say in which class you would expect to find the following books.

000	general	500	pure science
100	philosophy, psychology	600	applied science, technology
200	religion	700	arts, crafts, recreation
300	social science	800	literature
400	languages	900	geography, biography, history

- **(a)** A Guide To Opera
- **(b)** The Poems Of Shelley
- **(c)** Learning Business Japanese
- **(d)** A History Of The Arab Peoples
- **(e)** Sikhism
- **(f)** All About Computer Hacking
- **(g)** Modern Dance
- **(h)** The Bible
- **(i)** Mediterranean Cookery
- **(j)** The Rise And Fall of Adolf Hitler
- **(k)** The Life Of Martin Luther King
- **(l)** The Development Of Western Thought

'Finding your way round a library just takes a little practice.'

2* Put the following list of fiction authors into alphabetical order, as you would find them in a library.

- **(a)** John Wyndham
- **(b)** Roald Dahl
- **(c)** John Le Carré
- **(d)** Joan Lingard
- **(e)** Judith Kerr
- **(f)** C S Lewis
- **(g)** Rudyard Kipling
- **(h)** Sir Arthur Conan Doyle
- **(i)** Harper Lee
- **(j)** Mildred Taylor
- **(k)** George Orwell
- **(l)** Jonathan Swift
- **(m)** Graham Greene
- **(n)** Paul Zindel

'Fiction is arranged alphabetically by author.'

3* How much of a text do you understand? Do you read in depth, or just superficially? You probably do both. Sometimes we need to understand the complete meaning of the words and the

USING A LIBRARY
DO IT YOURSELF

consequences of them. At other times we want to dip into a book and get a flavour of it by reading a small part and predicting what the story is about. This helps us choose which books we want to read. We also use these *predictive skills* to enhance our enjoyment of a book, every time we find ourselves wondering what is going to happen next.

Read the following passages. 'The Life of a Princess' is taken from a modern children's novel, *No Need for Heroes* by Brian Keaney. 'The Life of a Pauper' is from a classic of English literature, *Oliver Twist* by Charles Dickens. Answer the questions that follow the passages, remembering to

- *answer fully:* You may be required to make more than one point or give more than one reason for what you say.
- *answer clearly:* Write in complete sentences, unless otherwise indicated.
- *give your reasons:* As with so much in English, there is not always just one correct reply to each question, so give the reasons for your opinion.

The Life of a Princess

Ariadne had not been very old when the news of her brother's death had been brought to the palace. But she could still remember it. She was standing on the beach in the full heat of the sun but the memory of that day made her shiver.

She hadn't liked him. She didn't like any of her brothers. They were all exactly like her father. They enjoyed fighting and killing. Most of the time they were off making war on some unsuspecting people, only returning once or twice a year covered in blood and dirt. Then there would be a few weeks of drunken feasting – the palace and all the out-houses filled with filthy soldiers, yelling, singing and brawling, her father in the middle of them with his arm around his son.

On that particular day, when the news came that his favourite son had been murdered, he had been entertaining the merchants of Crete. Fat old men in rich clothes, they sat around the table stuffing themselves with food and wine. The din of their laughter and shouting drowned the sound of the musicians who stood in one corner, playing. The room was hot and smoky. Servants went in and out carrying away dishes, bringing more food, passing the wine jug.

At the head of the table her father, King Minos of Crete, looked down on the company and smiled. He liked to see their greedy eyes turned towards him, ready to laugh at his jokes, ready to praise him for his generosity. His face was flushed with wine and he held a leg of chicken in one hand.

A messenger entered the room, a thin pale man. He looked nervously about him and then made his way slowly to the head of the table. He bowed before Minos, who tore with his teeth at the chicken leg and then graciously inclined his ear. The messenger whispered the news.

The colour drained from the king's face. He spat his meat across the table, opened his mouth wide and bellowed like a bull. All talking stopped in the hall as the merchants gazed fearfully at Minos. For a moment the musicians alone could be heard playing in the silence. Then they too stopped.

The Life Of A Pauper

The room in which the boys were fed was a large stone hall, with a copper at one end; out of which the master, dressed in an apron for the purpose, and assisted by one or two women, ladled the gruel at meal-times. Of this festive composition each boy had one porringer, and no more – except on occasions of great public rejoicing, when he had two ounces and a quarter of bread besides. The bowls never wanted washing. The boys polished them with their spoons till they shone again; and when they had performed this operation (which never took very long, the spoons being nearly as large as the bowls), they would sit staring at the copper, with such eager eyes, as if they could have devoured the very bricks of which it was composed; employing themselves, meanwhile, in sucking their fingers most assiduously, with the view of catching up any stray splashes of gruel that might have been cast thereon. Boys have generally excellent appetites. Oliver Twist and his companions suffered the tortures of slow starvation for three months. At last they got so voracious and wild with hunger, that one boy who was tall for his age, and hadn't been used to that sort of thing (for his father had kept a small cook's shop), hinted darkly to his companions, that unless he had another basin of gruel per diem [per day], he was afraid he might some night happen to eat the boy who slept next him, who happened to be a weakly youth of tender age. He had a wild, hungry eye ; and they implicitly believed him. A council was held;

USING A LIBRARY
DO IT YOURSELF

lots were cast who should walk up to the master after supper that evening and ask for more ; and it fell to Oliver Twist.

The evening arrived, the boys took their places. The master, in his cook's uniform, stationed himself at the copper ; his pauper assistants ranged themselves behind him; the gruel was served out; and a long grace was said over the short commons. The gruel disappeared; the boys whispered to each other, and winked at Oliver; while his next neighbours nudged him. Child as he was, he was desperate with hunger, and reckless with misery. He rose from the table; and advancing to his master, basin and spoon in hand, said, somewhat alarmed at his own temerity:

'Please, sir, I want some more.'

The master was a fat, healthy man; but he turned very pale. He gazed in stupefied astonishment on the small rebel for some seconds; and then clung for support to the copper. The assistants were paralyzed with wonder, the boys with fear.

'What!' said the master at length, in a faint voice.

'Please sir,' replied Oliver, 'I want some more'.

(a) 'The Life of a Princess'
  (i) What sort of a person was King Minos? Give examples of his behaviour that support your view.
  (ii) What are 'merchants' (line 14)? Why do you think King Minos was entertaining them?
  (iii) What do you think King Minos did next? What reasons can you give for your suggestion?

(b) 'The Life of a Pauper'
  (i) The boys are in a workhouse. How are they treated there?
  (ii) Why do the boys polish their bowls till they shine?
  (iii) Why do you think they are living in the workhouse?
  (iv) What does the author mean by the phrase 'somewhat alarmed at his own temerity' (line 35)?

(c) Both texts
  (i) What similarities are there between Ariadne's childhood and Oliver's? What differences?
  (ii) Explain how power is abused in each extract.
  (iii) Comment on how in both pieces an atmosphere of fear is built up.

4 Continue the story of 'The Life of a Princess' in exercise 3 in your own way.

SECTION 6

Tools for English

To make sense, words have to work together. To use language accurately and effectively, you need to understand the basic rules.

Parts of speech

Every word has its own function in a sentence, and these different functions each have different names. Some of the most important are *nouns, adjectives, verbs* and *adverbs*.

Nouns

Nouns are naming words. They are used to name:

someone	*boy, girl, clown, driver*
something	*desk, bucket, book, cake*
a place	*beach, street, city, countryside*

Singular and plural Nouns change according to whether they are naming one thing or a number of things – called the *singular* and *plural* forms.

boy singular *boys* plural

CONTENTS

Parts of speech

❖

Sentence grammar

❖

Spelling

❖

Punctuation

73

TOOLS FOR ENGLISH

PARTS OF SPEECH

There are four kinds of noun: *common, proper, collective* and *abstract*.
Common nouns are the names of ordinary, everyday people, places or objects. All of the examples given above are common nouns. We probably use this kind of noun more than any other kind, which is why they are called *common*.
Proper nouns These are the actual names of people or places. *America, George Washington, Taj Mahal* and *Gandhi* are all proper nouns, and have capital letters.
Collective nouns refer to groups of people or things. For example, we talk about a *herd* of cows, a library of books.
Abstract nouns are names for things that cannot be seen, touched, tasted, heard or smelt. For example, *beauty* is a thing but you cannot pick it up. *Peace* is another example; it cannot be seen or held, and yet we all know what it is. This is because it really exists in people's minds. Words like this are called abstract nouns.

Can you tell an abstract noun from a common noun? See how well you know your nouns. Do Exercise 1 of Do It Yourself on page 88.

Pronouns

Pronouns are words that take the place of nouns. There are a number of different kinds of pronoun.
Personal pronouns These are perhaps the simplest pronouns. Here are some examples:

    I me she her he him it we us you they them

Which pronoun you use depends on whether the thing you are talking about is the subject or the object (see pages 78–79).
Possessive pronouns The personal pronouns listed above also have a possessive form, to be used when something belongs to someone.
    The following chart shows both types of personal pronoun and the corresponding possessive pronouns. (The first of the pair of possessive pronouns is used with a noun, e.g. That is *my* table. The second is used on its own, e.g. That table is *mine*.)

Subjective pronoun	*Objective pronoun*	*Possessive pronoun*
I	me	my/mine
you	you	your/yours
he	him	his/his
she	her	her/hers
it	it	its
we	us	our/ours
they	them	their/theirs

SECTION 6
PARTS OF SPEECH

Interrogative pronouns These pronouns ask questions, e.g. *Which* of you is responsible?
    Other examples of interrogative pronouns are *who, whom, whose, which, what.*
Relative pronouns Some pronouns help to connect, or relate, one part of a sentence to another, so they are known as *relative pronouns*.
    The fire, *which* had been dying down for some time, finally went out.

As you can see, the same word can be an interrogative pronoun in one sentence and a relative pronoun in another. This is because how we describe a word depends on its function in a sentence.
    Other examples of relative pronouns include *who, whom, whose, which, that, what.*
Reflexive pronouns These refer, or reflect, back to nouns or pronouns that have already been used in the sentence.
    The meal, *itself*, was very good, but I didn't like the restaurant.
    I, *myself*, think the situation has gone too far.

Demonstrative pronouns point out a specific thing or things, e.g. Whose gloves are *these*?
    Other examples are *this, that* and *those*.
Indefinite pronouns refer to people or things without being definite or specific.
    I haven't got *any*.

Some, either, neither, none and *anything* are other examples.

Hunt the pronoun! Try Exercise 2 on page 88 of Do It Yourself.

Adjectives

Adjectives are used to describe nouns; they add details.
    a dog   a black *dog*

Black is an adjective. It tells us something about the dog.
An adjective is usually used in front of a noun. However, it can also be used with a verb (see page 76).
    Adjectives have two other forms which you should know about. These are called *comparatives* and *superlatives*.
Comparative adjectives are used to compare two things. They are normally formed by adding *-er* on to the end of an adjective. For instance, *smaller* is the comparative of the adjective *small*.
    This dog is *smaller* than that one.

'Adjectives add to our knowledge about nouns.'

75

TOOLS FOR ENGLISH
PARTS OF SPEECH

Superlative adjectives are used to compare three or more things. For example, *smallest* is the superlative of *small*.
> This dog is the *smallest* of all.

In general, comparatives are formed by adding *-er* and superlatives are formed by adding *-est* to the adjective. However, if an adjective already ends in *-e*, *-r* is added to form the comparative and *-st* to form the superlative.
> adjective *large*   comparative *larger*   superlative *largest*

When a word ends in *-y*, the comparative and superlative are formed by changing the *-y* to *-i* and adding *-er* for the comparative and *-est* for the superlative.
> adjective *happy*   comparative *happier*   superlative *happiest*

However, some comparatives and superlatives do not follow any of these rules. These, unfortunately, have to be learned. Here are two examples:
> adjective *good*   comparative *better*   superlative *best*
> adjective *bad*   comparative *worse*   superlative *worst*

There are also some words which do not sound right when *-er* or *-est* are added, and therefore use *more* and *most* instead.
> adjective *beautiful*   comparative *more beautiful*   superlative *most beautiful*

Verbs

Verbs express action. They tell us what people and things do. In the following example, *ate* is the verb.
> The black dog *ate* the bone.

Verbs also express existence, a state of *being*. Here *are* is the verb:
> Those *are* my shoes.

Verbs like *are, is, was, were, seems, looks* and *feels* are often used together with adjectives:
> I feel good.
> The singer was terrible.

'The verb is the most important part of any sentence. It tells us what a person or thing is doing.'

SECTION 6
PARTS OF SPEECH

Verbs can be much more complicated than other words because they change according to the time of the action they are describing. Different forms of the verb are used to describe:
- an action in the present
- an action in the past
- an action in the future.

These different forms are called the *present tense, past tense,* and *future tense*.

Present tense	I sing, I am singing
Past tense	I was singing, I sang, I have sung
Future tense	I will sing, I shall sing, I am going to sing

A verb performs the most important function in a sentence because without a verb a sentence does not make sense.
   The girl the piano (without a verb)
   The girl played the piano. (with a verb)

> *A verb can be made up of more than one word.*

Adverbs

Adverbs are used to add details to the actions described by verbs. Here, *greedily* is the adverb:
   He ate *greedily*.

Adverbs can often be made from adjectives, simply by adding *-ly*.
   adjective *greedy*   adverb *greedily*

We use different kinds of adverb to tell us *how, when* or *where* something happened. We call these adverbs of *manner,* adverbs of *time* and adverbs of *place*. In the following example, *noisily* is an adverb of manner.
   The boy whistled *noisily*.

Yesterday is an adverb of time.
   The dog went missing *yesterday*.

Here is an adverb of place.
   The boy brought the dog *here*.

> *Adverbs add to our knowledge about verbs. They tell us when, where and how verbs take place.*

77

Adverbs can also be used in conjunction with adjectives to make them weaker or stronger. Here, *appallingly* and *very* are adverbs:
>The concert was *appallingly* bad.
>The child was *very* ill.

Prepositions

Prepositions are words which show the relationship between things. They tell you that something is, for example, *over, under, inside* or *beside* something else. Prepositions always relate nouns or pronouns to other words in the sentence. Pronouns that follow prepositions should be objective (see page 74).

Sentence grammar

It is important to understand the basic principles of sentence grammar. This means the rules governing the way that sentences are put together. To understand the rules, you need to know about the *subject* and the *object*.

The subject

The subject of a sentence is the person or thing doing the action:
>*The boy* was swimming.

Another way of expressing the same thing is to say that the subject is the noun (boy) governing the verb (was swimming).
   A subject can also be a pronoun:
>*He* was swimming.

Phrases

Every sentence needs a subject and a verb. If a group of words does not have these, we refer to them as a *phrase*.
>singing in the rain

Clauses

A group of words which has a verb and subject is known as a *clause*.
>*He* (subject) *ate* (verb) the cheese.

A clause can either be a sentence on its own, like the preceding example, or be part of a more complex sentence.

> He ate the cheese because he was hungry.

In this example there are two clauses. The first one, *he ate the cheese*, is called the *main clause*, because it provides us with the main piece of information in the sentence. The second clause, *because he was hungry*, is known as a *subordinate clause*, because it is of lesser importance. Unlike the main clause, it could not make up a sentence on its own and depends on the main clause to complete its meaning.

The object

The object is the person or thing affected by the action of the verb:

> She threw the ball.

In this example *the ball* is the object. Every sentence needs a subject, but not every sentence needs an object. In the sentence above, *the ball* is a *direct object*. It is directly affected by the action of the verb; in other words, it has the action of the verb done to it. Sometimes a verb can affect something or someone indirectly:

> He gave *me* the ball.

In this example the *ball* is the **direct object** and *me* is the **indirect object**. You cannot have an indirect object without a direct object as well.

Spelling

Words are made up of *syllables*. A syllable is the smallest unit of pronunciation into which a word can be broken down:

> *unfortunately* has 5 syllables   un-for-tu-nate-ly

If you are uncertain how to spell a word, it helps to break it down into its syllables and try to spell each one separately. However, there are also a number of spelling aids which you can use to help you.

Learning spellings

One way to deal with spelling problems is to learn the correct spellings. You need to be quite deliberate about this. It is no good just looking at

'Have a dictionary at home, and know how to use it.'

SECTION **6**
SPELLING

79

TOOLS FOR ENGLISH
SPELLING

the word for a minute and hoping that you have learnt it. Follow this method:

- **Look** up the correct spelling of the word in a dictionary.
- **Say** the spelling out loud to yourself over and over again.
- **Cover** over the word and try to spell it correctly. If you are not absolutely certain of how it should be spelt, spend some more time learning.
- **Write** it out to test yourself.
- **Check** to see if you are right.

Homophones

Unfortunately, there are a number of words in the English language which sound the same or very similar, but which have different meanings and are spelt differently. We call words like this *homophones*. Here are some common homophones which it is easy to confuse.

right	correct, opposite of left	That is the *right* answer.
write	what you do with a pen	I am going to *write* a letter.
wood	where trees grow	She was lost in the *wood*.
would	might possibly	I *would* go home if I had the money.
no	negative	I have *no* money.
know	understand	I *know* how to drive.
too	more than expected	It is *too* dark.
two	a number	I have *two* eyes.
to	a direction	I went *to* the party.
	or part of a verb	I want *to* eat.
hear	listen to a sound	I can *hear* voices.
here	a place	They are over *here*.
their	belonging to them	It is *their* house.
there	a place	Put it *there*.
they're	short for 'they are'	She said, '*They're* all here.'
where	a question	*Where* were you?
wear	what you do with clothes	I think I will *wear* a coat.
we're	short for 'we are'	They said, '*We're* fed up.'
whose	belonging to whom	*Whose* coat is this?
who's	short for 'who is'	*Who's* coming to dinner?'

SECTION 6
SPELLING

accept	to receive something	I *accepted* his apology.
except	to exclude something	She eats all fruit *except* bananas.
principal	the head of a college	I have to go and see the *principal*.
principle	a belief or idea	Eating meat is against my *principles*.
off	not on	She got *off* the bus.
of	relating to something	A game *of* football

Note: *Of* is sometimes incorrectly used instead of *have*. In speech we often shorten the word *have*:

I should*'ve* done my homework

instead of

I should *have* done my homework.

It is easy to fall into the mistake of writing *should of* for *should've*.

Prefixes and suffixes

Sometimes a word is added to in a way that changes both the spelling and the meaning. When the addition comes at the beginning of a word, it is called a *prefix*; when it comes at the end, it is known as a *suffix*.

If you understand the meaning of prefixes and suffixes, it will help you not to misspell. Here are a few of the more common prefixes:

ante-	before	antechamber, antenatal
anti-	against	antisocial, antiseptic
auto-	self	autobiography, automatic
dis-	not, away	disapprove, disarm
inter-	between	international
mis-	wrong	misspell, misplace
pre-	before	prefix, precondition
pro-	for, forward	pronoun, progress
sub-	under	submarine
super-	above, beyond	superhuman, supersonic
tele-	from afar	telepathic
un-	not, in reverse	unjust, undo

81

When the last letter of a prefix is the same as the first letter of the word, then there will be a double letter:
> dis+solve dissolve, mis+spell misspell

Below are some common *suffixes* you will no doubt have come across:

-able	likely to,	adaptable
-ible	able to	accessible
-ful	full of, having the character of	beautiful, truthful
-ist	one who practises, works with	physicist, dentist
-ly	state or quality	daintily evidently
-ward	towards	backward, forward
-wards		

Spelling rules

There are some spelling rules which you can learn, but it is important to realise that spelling rules never work all the time. There are always exceptions.

drop the -e before -ing When you need to add *-ing* to a verb that ends in *-e*, drop the *-e* first.
> *bake* becomes *baking*; *file* becomes *filing*

i* before *e*, except after *c This rule works in most cases.
> *believe* (*i* before *e*); *receive* (*e* before *i* after *c*)

As with most rules, there are some exceptions, (e.g. seize, protein), and there is no alternative but to learn these.

Forming plurals

When you are changing words to their plural forms, the spelling also changes. Sometimes this is quite straightforward; at other times it is more complicated.

Plurals with *-es* Most nouns form their plural by adding *-s*. However, words that already end in *-s*, and words ending in *-x*, *-z*, *-ch* and *-sh* all add *-es* in the plural. For example:

singular	plural
gas	gases
fox	foxes
buzz	buzzes
lunch	lunches
fish	fishes

Plural of words ending in -o Words that end in -o can form their plural either by adding -s or -es. The more modern words, like photo or dynamo, tend to add -s. There is no actual rule, and you need to learn which is which.

singular	plural	singular	plural
potato	potatoes	photo	photos
tomato	tomatoes	piano	pianos
cargo	cargoes	dynamo	dynamos
volcano	volcanoes	solo	solos

Plural of words ending in -f, -fe or -ff Most words ending in -f, -fe or -ff drop the -f to form their plural, and add -ves:

singular	plural
leaf	leaves
wolf	wolves

There are a few which just add -s. The commonest of these are:

singular	plural
chief	chiefs
proof	proofs
roof	roofs
belief	beliefs
grief	griefs

One word, dwarf, can form its plural either way: dwarf (singular), dwarfs or dwarves (plural).

Plural of words ending in -y Words ending in -y can form their plural in one of two ways. If there is a vowel before the -y, then you need to add -s:

singular	plural
donkey	donkeys

83

But if the letter before the -y is a consonant, you need to change the -y to -i and add -es.

singular	plural
country	countries

Nouns and verbs

Some nouns and verbs are almost identical, except for one letter (-s or -c). These are words like *practice* and *practise*. In this case, the rule is that the noun ends in -ce and the verb ends in -se:

noun	verb
practice	practise
licence	license

This is clearer if you think of the words advice (noun) and advise (verb). In this case you can actually hear the difference.

Another pair of words that are often confused are *affect* and *effect*.
   affect is the verb: The smoke *affected* my voice.
   effect is usually a noun: It had a bad *effect* on me.

Punctuation

In order to produce written English that other people can understand, we have to make use of punctuation marks and conventions.

Capital letters

Capital letters are used for proper nouns and for titles, e.g. *Mickey Mouse, the Pope, the Eiffel Tower, Winston Churchill*. They are also used at the beginning of sentences and for the first word in direct speech (dialogue):
   He looked up at me and said, '**D**o you know who I am?'

Note: The word *I*, meaning 'myself', is always written as a capital letter.

Full-stops, question marks, exclamation marks

Ordinary full stops (.) are used at the ends of sentences. If a sentence is a question, we use a *question mark* (?). If we wish to add emphasis to a sentence, we use an *exclamation mark* (!).

Have you absorbed enough about spelling? See what you can remember by doing Exercises 3 and 4 on pages 88–89 of Do It Yourself.

❝ *Don't overdo exclamation marks or you will lessen their impact.* ❞

Commas

Commas (,) are used for a variety of purposes, one of which is to act as separators. They divide a sentence into units.

Lists A sentence that contains a list needs commas to separate the individual items: e.g. He bought bread, biscuits, tea and oranges. (You do not need a comma to separate the last two items; the word *and* acts as a separator.)

Direct speech Commas are also used in direct speech to separate the words spoken from words which tell us who said them:

> Emma said, 'I am going to the cinema.'
> 'I am going to the cinema,' Emma said.

Apposition Commas are used to separate nouns or phrases from other words which explain them:

> Harry Staines, the Crawford striker, was sent off the field for a foul.

Harry Staines and *the Crawford striker* are the same person, so *the Crawford striker* is said to be in apposition to *Harry Staines*.

Subordinate clauses When a subordinate clause is placed before a main clause (see page 79), the clauses are separated by a comma:

> Because he was hungry, he ate the cheese

Relative clauses, which are introduced by a relative pronoun (see page 75), are separated from the rest of the sentence by commas:

> The reporter, who had been waiting for hours, finally went home.

However, if the clause is essential to the sense of the sentence, then commas are not used:

> The reporter who had witnessed the crime was asked to give evidence.

In this case, the clause tells us which particular reporter was asked to give evidence. It *is*, therefore, essential to the sense of the sentence.

Asides Commas are also used to mark off *asides*. These are words such as *however*, *indeed* or *nevertheless*:

> It is, therefore, essential to the sense of the sentence.

Colons

A colon is used to break up a sentence when the second part of it explains, expands or summarises the first part:

> Finally she told us what was in the box: a live snake.

> *If you can use a full stop, you should not use a comma.*

SECTION 6
PUNCTUATION

Colons are also used to introduce lists:
> Rubbish was lying everywhere: potato peelings, rotten fruit, tea-bags and newspapers.

Semi-colons

A semi-colon is used to join together two very closely linked sentences:
> I never exercise; that is why I am slightly overweight.

It is also used to separate items in a list of phrases or clauses:
> At the zoo we saw: a tiger eating some raw meat; an elephant splashing water; lots of small black fish swimming around in shoals; and chimpanzees having their afternoon tea.

Note that the list in the above example is introduced by a colon. Note also that, unlike the comma, a semi-colon *is* normally used before a final *and*.

Dashes

Dashes are often used in direct speech or in writing stories which have a conversational tone.

Double dashes Pairs of dashes are sometimes used instead of commas:
> Last night I saw Ahmed – the boy I met at the disco – and we went skating.

Single dashes On its own, a dash can be used to show a change or break in thought:
> Just as we believed ourselves safer – but I'll tell you about that later.

'Dashes should be used sparingly.'

Apostrophes

There are two kinds of apostrophe ('): the apostrophe of *possession* and the apostrophe of *omission*.

omission The apostrophe of omission is used to show that a letter (or letters) has been left out. We often need to leave out letters when we are writing out speech, in which people commonly use shortened forms of verbs, such as *we're* meaning *we are*, or *she's* meaning *she is*.

possession This apostrophe shows that one thing belongs to another or to a person or place:

The horse's mane	the mane belonging to the horse
Stephen's house	the house belonging to Stephen
Scotland's lakes	the lakes belonging to Scotland

SECTION 6
PUNCTUATION

It shows possession or ownership, with the apostrophe coming *immediately* after the owner word, whether that word is singular or plural:

>Have you seen the woman's new hairstyle? (the hairstyle of one woman)
>Have you seen the women's new hairstyles? (the hairstyles of two or more women)
>
>The garden's lawn is looking very luxuriant. (the lawn of one garden)
>The gardens' lawns are looking very luxuriant. (the lawns of two or more gardens)

Quotation marks

If you quote from something someone says, you should put it in *quotation marks* (' ' or " "), also known as inverted commas.

A quotation can be very obvious. If, for example, you were writing a report on a football match and the goalkeeper had said, 'It was a nightmare. It was the worst day of my life', you might write:

>On a day that goalkeeper, Henry Lawson, described as 'a nightmare' and 'the worst day of my life', Brockley United crashed to a 3–0 defeat.

A quotation can also be less obvious. For example, an American high-jumper called Fosbury was the first to develop the method of high-jumping with one's back to the bar. Somebody named this jump the 'Fosbury Flop'. Because it was something someone had said, it was written in quotation marks.

It is only when a phrase like this stops being thought of as something someone said, and becomes accepted as a part of the language, that people stop putting it in quotation marks.

Names of things that have been invented and titles of books, films or plays should also be written in inverted commas:

>Shakespeare's play, 'Macbeth', is a tragedy.

In print, italics are sometimes used instead of quotation marks:

>Shakespeare's play, *Macbeth*, is a tragedy.

Quotation marks, sometimes referred to as **speech marks**, are also used for dialogue. When you are writing a story, you may wish to include characters who speak. The rules for punctuating dialogue are explained on page 56.

A final exercise to test your punctuation skills: Exercise 5 of Do It Yourself, on page 89.

87

TOOLS FOR ENGLISH
DO IT YOURSELF

Do It Yourself

Exercises marked with a * have answers, or suggested answers, in the Answers section at the back of the book.

1* How many different kinds of

  (a) abstract nouns
  (b) common nouns
  (c) proper nouns

can you find in the following passage?

> *There was only one hope left: the skylight. If he could somehow force it open and get out onto the roof, there was a chance of escaping that way. He picked up the handle of the broom and jabbed it upwards. It was hopeless. The glass of the skylight seemed as strong as concrete. James felt full of a deep despair. He would die in here. No one would ever know the truth. If only he had listened to Maggie. Was it only last Monday that she wanted him to forget about the empty house? It seemed like an eternity now.*

2* Can you find the pronouns in the following sentences?

  (a) I painted the room myself.
  (b) Which of you is the tallest?
  (c) Whom do I have the honour of addressing?
  (d) You are standing on my toe!
  (e) This is the best that money can buy.

3* Turn these words into their opposites by adding a prefix:

  (a) expensive   (e) ability   (i) known
  (b) appear   (f) understand   (j) approve
  (c) happy   (g) necessary   (k) possible
  (d) visible   (h) infect   (l) likely

'*Don't reject the right word just because you don't know how to spell it.*'

88

SECTION 6
DO IT YOURSELF

4 * Write the plurals of the following words:

(a) video   (e) family   (i) thief
(b) half   (f) shampoo   (j) studio
(c) loaf   (g) monkey   (k) bus
(d) library   (h) alley   (l) coach

5 Punctuating properly is a part of writing. The more you write and look at what you write, the more you will develop your own punctuation skills. Here are two exercises to help you practise:

(a) How does your punctuation compare with published work?
Stage one Write a short story on a subject and for an audience of your own choosing.
Stage two Now choose a novel or book of short stories which you have read and enjoyed. Compare the way a page of each is punctuated.
- What similarities are there?
- What differences are there?
- What have you learned from the comparison?

(b) How much difference does your punctuation make?
Stage one Write a talk for a partner to read aloud on one of the following subjects:
  Modern education
  People's prejudices
  What people should aim for in life
Stage two When you have written it out, ask your friend to read it through and discuss with you anything that is unclear.
Stage three Rewrite your talk in the light of your friend's comments.
Stage four Decide how many of your friend's queries were caused by unclear expressions and how many by poor punctuation.

'Choosing which punctuation is correct needs practice and more practice.'

Answers

Section 1

1 You could have found a large number of words. Here are some of the possibilities.
  (a) script, describe, prescribe, prescription, inscribe, inscription
  (b) conduct, conductor, reduce, induce, produce
  (c) deposit, postpone, position, imposition
  (d) credible, incredible, credulous, incredulous, credit, creed

2 (a) The First Witch had been 'killing swine'.
  (b) The woman would not give the witch any of her chestnuts. Instead she told her to go away.
  (c) Her husband's ship was called the 'Tiger'.
  (d) Each of the witches offers to give a wind.
  (e) The First Witch uses a 'pilot's thumb' in her spell.
  (f) The spell will make the sailor unable to sleep. As a result he will waste away.
  (g) The spell will cause his ship to be tossed about by storms.
  (h) The witches are called 'posters of the sea and land' because 'posters' means swift travellers and they fly over both the sea and the land.
  (i) In the last six lines the language becomes repetitive, suggesting a charm or spell.
  (j) To seal their spell, the witches join hands and dance nine times in a circle.

3 (a) A usurper is someone who seizes another person's throne or title. The usurper was the duke's brother, who had stolen his title and banished him.
  (b) His friends had chosen of their own free will to go into exile with the duke.
  (c) 'Habit' is another word for 'custom'.
  (d) When people talk about 'a golden age' they usually mean a perfect time in the past. The authors' idea of a golden age was a time when people lived carefree lives in the forests of England.
  (e) The 'poor dappled fools' are the deer. They are 'poor' because they are going to be eaten.
  (f) The duke's followers were so fond of the deer that they did not want to kill them for meat.
  (g) 'When the cold winds of winter made the duke feel the change of his adverse fortune' means 'when the cold winter winds brought it home to the duke how his life had been unfairly changed'.

ANSWERS
SECTION 1

4 one of Her Majesty's guests a prisoner
a drop too much drunk
gone to a better place died
the smallest room the lavatory
hard of hearing deaf
invited to offer one's resignation sacked
off colour sick
a little shy of the truth lying

5 **decibel** the unit for measuring sound, the bel, was named after Alexander Graham Bell (1847–1922), inventor of the telephone. A decibel is a tenth of a bel.
guillotine Dr Joseph Guillotin (1738–1814) suggested that Frenchmen who had been sentenced to death should be beheaded. The actual machine for doing this was invented by one of his pupils.
boycott Charles Cunningham Boycott (1832–97) was a landowner in Ireland who was hated so much by his tenants that they refused to work for him or even talk to him.
diesel the diesel engine was named after its inventor, Rudolf Diesel (1858–1913).
mesmerise Franz Mesmer (1734–1815) was one of the first people to experiment with hypnotism and believed that he could use it to cure disease. He was eventually exposed as a fraud, but his experiments led others to look more closely at the phenomenon.
chauvinist Nicholas Chauvin was a soldier in Napoleon's army. His patriotism was so extreme that his name became used for people who put their country above all else. Later, men who thought of things only from the male point of view, became known as male chauvinists.
pasteurise Louis Pasteur (1822–95) is regarded as the father of bacteriology. He invented a way of sterilisation by heating.
hoover William H. Hoover (1849–1932) did not invent the vacuum cleaner. He bought the rights to the invention from a Mr Spangler and his company was so successful that people called the machines after him.
tarmac John Loudon McAdam (1756–1836) invented a method of surfacing roads using crushed stones, known as macadamising. Tar-macadamising was a later development, using tar. This was later shortened to tarmac.
leotard Jules Leotard (1842–70) was a French trapeze artist who wore a type of skin-tight garment during his act.

ANSWERS

SECTIONS 1–2

6 *panama* straw hat named after a Central American country, Panama
balaclava woollen helmet named after Balaklava in Russia
duffel coat or bag named after the town Duffel in Belgium
muslin cloth named after the town of Mosul in Iraq
bikini bathing costume named after the island of Bikini in the Pacific Ocean
jodhpurs riding trousers named after the town of Jodhpur in India
cashmere a soft wool named after the Kashmir region in India

Section 2

1 (a) fact (b) opinion (c) fact
(d) opinion (e) fact (f) opinion
(g) opinion (h) fact (i) opinion
(j) fact

2 (a) It does not make clear *which* people prefer it or *to what* they prefer it.
(b) Who carried out the research? When and where was it carried out? How many people were questioned? Was it a representative sample of the population? What questions were they asked?
(c) There are a number of unusual language features, including:
rhyme – shifty/nifty
alliteration – product/prefer, stubborn/stains
'the product that people prefer' is a catch-phrase
(d) 'Unique' means that there is nothing else like it. The phrase 'unique formula' suggests that no other product uses the same mixture of ingredients. To test this claim, you would need to compare the formula to that of other stain removers, either by reading the list of ingredients, if there were one, or by having it analysed in a laboratory.
(e) For it to be a 'bargain' price it ought to be cheaper than other, similar products, or cheaper than the price at which it was previously on sale.

3 positive: shrewed, inquiring, displaying, confident, tact, information, regular, sacrifice, meticulous, childlike
negative: dishonest, suspicious, showing off, arrogant, deceit, propaganda, monotonous, waste, fussy, childish

92

Section 3

2 The items you might want to put on your agenda could include some or all of the following:
  - **(a)** What are the problems?
    Who are the groups responsible for problems?
    What possible solutions are there?
    How could posters help?
    What messages could posters carry?
    Where should posters be placed?
  - **(b)** Who should be invited?
    Where will the party be held?
    What food and drink can be provided?
    Will there be music?
    How long will it last?
    Who will clear up afterwards?
  - **(c)** What are the dates of the trip?
    What is the destination?
    What are the accommodation arrangements?
    How will the group travel to its destination?
    What will each individual need for the journey?
    How much will it cost?
  - **(d)** (Assuming the play has been decided on)
    Who will direct the play?
    What parts should each actor take?
    What other jobs need to be done to produce the play?
    Where can any props/scenery etc. be found?
    How much time is needed to prepare and rehearse?
    How often will rehearsals be held?
    What days/nights will performances be on?
    Where will the performance(s) be?
    How many performances?
    Who will the audience be?
    How will the play be publicised?
    Will the audience be charged for admission?
  - **(e)** Can he/she play or sing well?
    Does he/she have the right equipment?
    Would he/she fit into the group?
    Does he/she have the time to make a regular commitment?
    Is he/she prepared to work as hard as the other group members?

ANSWERS

SECTIONS 4–5

Section 4

3 Everyone's report will be different. There is no correct answer. However, it is possible to make mistakes by not using indirect speech correctly. Here is an example of how it might be done.

Ron Stafford, chairman of Drakeham United, called a surprise press-conference this morning to launch a bombshell on the world of professional football. He looked tired and strained and wasted little time on preliminaries, other than to thank reporters for turning up at short notice.

His purpose in calling in the press, he said, was to let the public know what had been going on at the club. He said he wanted to emphasise that it had all been happening behind his back.

Apparently, last week he overheard two of his players talking in the locker rooms after the match. They talked about the match being fixed and about the goal-keeper being paid three thousand pounds to let a shot into the net. They also discussed smaller payments to other players. Ron said he had got the impression that this had been going on for some time.

Questions were fired at the beleaguered chairman from all sides but he would say little else, only adding that an emergency meeting of the directors had been held at which the manager and all the players were interviewed and that the manager, goalkeeper and three other players had been suspended pending further enquiries.

Section 5

1 (a) 700 (b) 800 (c) 400 (d) 900
(e) 200 (f) 600 (g) 700 (h) 200
(i) 700 (j) 900 (k) 900 (l) 100

2 1(h) 2(b) 3(m) 4(e) 5(g) 6(c) 7(i)
8(f) 9(d) 10(k) 11(l) 12(j) 13(a) 14(n)

3 a (i) King Minos was a brutal man. The narrator tells us that when he returned from battle 'there would be a few weeks of drunken feasting – the palace and all the outhouses filled with filthy soldiers, yelling, singing and brawling', with 'her father in the middle of them'.
(ii) 'Merchants' are people who buy and sell goods. The merchants of Crete were probably among its wealthier and more important citizens. King Minos was entertaining them because he enjoyed displaying his power over them.
(iii) He clearly did something violent. We know that he was a violent man and that he loved his son. He was obviously greatly affected by the news the messenger brought him.

b (i) Life in the workhouse is very harsh. The boys, who take their meals together, are given very little to eat and they live in fear.
(ii) The boys' behaviour with their bowls shows that they are ready to eat up the slightest scrap. It is proof that they are living at a level close to starvation.
(iii) They are living in the workhouse because they are 'paupers', or poor people, who cannot afford to support themselves.
(iv) By the phrase 'somewhat alarmed at his

ANSWERS
SECTIONS 5–6

own temerity' the author means 'rather frightened by his own rashness'.

c (i) Both Ariadne and Oliver live in an unhappy environment. Both are permanently frightened. Also, both of these extracts take place at mealtime. However, there are many differences. Ariadne lives in a wealthy household; her main problem is her relationship with her family. Oliver does not have a family. His main problem is getting enough to eat.

(ii) In the first extract King Minos is able to indulge his own lust for power, and to behave however he likes, without any rules except his own whims. In the second extract the system over which the Master of the Workhouse presides forces the children to beg for the food they need to survive, while condemning them for doing so.

(iii) You may wish to comment on
- how the opening paragraphs set the scene
- how people are described
- how people behave
- the language the writers use.

Section 6

1 abstract nouns   hope, chance, way, despair, truth, eternity
common nouns   skylight, roof, handle, broom, glass, concrete, house
proper nouns   James, Maggie, Monday

2 (a) I, myself   (b) which, you   (c) whom, I
(d) you, my   (e) this, that

3 (a) inexpensive   (b) disappear   (c) unhappy
(d) invisible   (e) inability (or disability)
(f) misunderstand   (g) unnecessary   (h) disinfect
(i) unknown   (j) disapprove
(k) impossible   (l) unlikely

4 (a) videos   (b) halves   (c) loaves
(d) libraries   (e) families   (f) shampoos
(g) monkeys   (h) alleys   (i) thieves
(j) studios   (k) buses   (l) coaches

95

NOTES

NOTES

NOTES

NOTES

NOTES

NOTES

NOTES

NOTES

NOTES

NOTES

NOTES

Index

A
abbreviations 52
accents 18–19
acronyms 17
adjectives 75–78
   comparative 75
   superlative 76
adverbs 77–78
advertisements 24–32, 44
   misleading 25
   reading 25, 27
agenda 35–36, 44
Alexandria, library of 13
alliteration 28
alphabetical order 47–49, 63
ambiguity 25
analysis 52
Anglo-Saxon 14
apostrophes 86–87
apposition 85
archives 59
articles, magazine 60
As You Like It 22
asides 85
association of ideas 26–27
association of words 17, 27–28, 30, 48
audience awareness 42, 45, 50, 53, 55
author 11, 63–72
autobiographies 49–50

B
Basque language 11
bias 26
biographies 49–50
books
   borrowing 61
   classification in libraries 62
   non-fiction 49, 61
   of quotations 49
   recommended 66–69
   reference 49–50
brainstorming 38

C
campaigning 35, 43
Canterbury Tales, The 15
capital letters 17, 84
   in speech 56–57
card index 59, 63
catalogue, library 63–64
catch-phrases 28, 32
Celtic languages 12–14
chair, role of 35, 38, 43
changes in language 10–23
chapters 50, 65
characters, creating 55–56
   in scripts 57
charts 53
Chaucer, Geoffrey 10, 15
children's fiction, modern 67–69
church language 12
class discussion 38
classical languages 12–13
classification of books 62
clauses 79, 85–86
   main 79
   relative 85
   subordinate 79, 85
closing sentence 50
code, language as 24
collating information 50
colon 85–86
commas 85
committee meetings 35–37, 43
communication 11, 16, 24, 33–45
   one-to-one 40
complex sentences 79
computer 47, 50, 55
conclusions 38, 50
consensus 37, 43
conditional tense 57
Constantinople, library of 13
contents 50, 65
conversation 18, 51, 57, 84
Cornish 12
criticism, constructive, of writing 54, 59
cross-references 48–49, 59

D
dash 86
data presentation 53
data processing 46
dead languages 16
decision-making 36
devices, in speech 28
Dewey Decimal System 62, 69
diagrams 53
   spider 42, 43
dialect 18–19
dialogue 57, 84, 87
diaries 50–51, 59
Dickens, Charles 70–71
dictionaries 47–48, 54, 79–80
   Oxford English Dictionary 17
direct speech 56, 84–86
discussion
   class 38
   group 34, 38, 43–44

INDEX

topic of 38
double letters 82
double negative 15
draft, final 54
drafting reports 54
drama 26

E

emphasis 84
encyclopaedia 49
English
　Middle 14–15
　Modern 14
　Old 13–15
　Standard 18–19
　words 10–23
eponyms 17, 23
ESL (English as a Second
　Language) 16
euphemisms 17, 18, 23
European languages 11–13
evolution of English 11
exclamation marks 84
extracts 15, 20, 70–71

F

facts, in advertising 26–27
family history 51, 59
feedback 43
fiction 63, 67
figures of speech 28
films 57, 87
formal groups 35–36
formal language 18, 33–34, 42, 53
French 11–14
full-stops 84
future tense 57, 77

G

Gaelic 11–12
German 11–12, 17
Germanic languages 12
grammar 15, 19, 78–79
Greek 11–13
　Ancient, 16
Greek alphabet 13
group discussion 34, 36–38, 43–44

groups 34
　formal 35–36
　informal 37

H

handwriting 54
headings 50–54, 59
　paragraphs 42
headwords 47–49
hieroglyphs 13
history books 49–50
homophones 80–81
hypotheses 52

I

idioms 16–17
illustrations 26, 50–54
imagery in stories 55
images
　in advertising 26–27
　on posters 28, 29
index 48, 59, 65
　card 59, 63
indirect speech, 56–57, 60
Indo-european languages 11, 19
informal groups 37
informal language 18, 33–34
information
　collating 50
　reading for 50
　researching 46
　retrieval 62
　sources 47–51
　storing 47
　written 26
initial letters 17
interviews 18, 40–41, 44, 51, 57
inverted commas (speech marks) 56–57, 87
inverting sentences 53
ISBN (International Standard Book Number) 64
Italic languages 12
italic print 87

J

jingles 28, 32
journalists 17
Joyce, James 53

K

key words 40, 50

L

Lamb, Charles and Mary 21
language
　as code 24
　Basque 11
　Celtic 12–14
　changes in 10–23
　church 12
　classical 12–13
　Cornish 12
　creating 16
　dead 16
　European 11–13
　families 11–12
　formal, 18, 33–34, 42, 53
　French 11–13
　Gaelic 11–12
　German 11–12
　Germanic 11–12
　Greek 11–13
　Indo-European 19
　influence of 14–15, 23–32
　informal 18, 33–34
　Italic 12
　Latin 11–13
　in law 34
　manipulating 28
　Middle English 14–15
　Modern English 14–16
　native 16
　Norman French 12
　Old English 13–15
　origins of 10–11
　patterns of 11
　of persuasion 24–32
　powers of 34
　register 19, 34
　Romance 12
　rules 73–89
　spoken 16
　Welsh 11
Latin 11–13
　roots 12–13, 19
　words 13, 16
law, language of 34
leader, group 37
letters 50–51, 59

108

INDEX

of alphabet 13
capital 17, 56, 84
double 82
initial 17
sounds of 13
level of formality 34
levels of meaning 24
libraries 13, 59–72
library catalogue 63–64
literary heritage 10, 65
literature
    pre-twentieth century 66
    twentieth century 66
Lord's Prayer, in Old English 14

M

Macbeth 20
magazines 44, 53
main clause 79
manuals 49
marks
    exclamation 84
    punctuation 84
    question 84
meaning
    levels of 24
    surface 25
    or words 19, 28, 47
meetings 44
messages, hidden, in advertising 26
microfiche 63
Middle Ages 13
Middle English 14–15
minutes of committee meetings 35–37
Modern English 14–16

N

names
    place 23
    product 30
narrative writing 55
native speaker 16
negative, double 15
negative associations 28, 30
negotiating skills 37
newspapers 53, 60
non-fiction books 49, 61, 63
non-Standard words 17
Norman French 12, 14
notes
    for reports 54
    for talk 45
    organising 59
    writing 37, 42, 51–52
nouns 47, 73–74, 78, 82–85, 88
    abstract 74, 88
    collective 74
    common 74, 88
    proper 74, 84, 88
novels 65–72, 89

O

object 79
    direct 79
    indirect 79
objectivity 26
observation 43
Old English 13–15
Oliver Twist 70–71
one-to-one communication 40
open-ended questions 40
opening sentence 50
opinions 26–27
oral evidence 51
order of text 50
origins
    of language 10–11
    of words 13
Oxford English Dictionary 17

P

page references 50, 65
pamphlets 29
paragraphs 50, 53–54, 56
    headings 42
parts of speech 47, 73
past tense 57, 77
paste-up 50
persuasion, language of 24–32
photocopies 50
photographs 51
phrases 85, 86, 78
pictograms 13
pictures 26
place names 23
planning
    meetings 43
reports 54
plays 44, 57–58
    Shakespeare's 11
    title 87
plenary session 38
plot of story 55
plurals 82–84, 89
poems 27
positive associations 28, 30
posters 29, 44
power of language 34
pre-writing a report 54
prefixes 81–82, 88
prepositions 78
presentation 42, 53, 54
presenting a talk 42, 45
present tense 57, 77
press conference 60
prioritising ideas 52–54
problem solving 38
processing data 46
product names 30
pronouns 74–75, 78, 88
    demonstrative 75
    indefinite 75
    interrogative 75
    personal 74
    possessive 74
    reflexive 75
    relative 75
pronunciation 17, 47, 79–80
publishing 44, 64
punctuation 52, 54, 84–86, 88–89

Q

questions 57
    on agenda 44
    in interviews 40–41
    open-ended 40
question marks 84
questionnaire 41, 44
quotation marks (speech marks) 56–57, 87
quotation 49, 56–57, 87

R

reading
    advertisements 25, 27
    drafts 54
    in depth 69

INDEX

for enjoyment 55
for information 50
programmes 65
recommended 66–68
scanning books 50, 64
skim 50
record
  family 51
  of books read 66
  written 47
reference, page 50, 65
reference books 49–50
register, language 18–19, 34
rehearsing a talk 45
relative clauses 85
Renaissance 13
repetition 28
reported speech 56
reporting 36, 46–60
reports
  notes for 54
  structure of 52, 59
  writing 51–53, 59, 87
research 46–60, 64
rhyme 28
Roman culture 12–13
Romance languages 12
Romeo and Juliet 15
roots, Latin 12–13, 19
rules
  grammar 15
  spelling 82–84

S

sampling text 64
sayings 16
scanning
  books 64
  text 50
scientific words 13
scribe 37–38
scripted speech 56–57
scripts 57–58
secretary 35, 37, 43
section headings 54
semi-colon 86
sentences
  breaking up 85
  clauses in 79
  closing 50
  complex 79

end of 84
inverting 53
length of 54
linked 86
opening 50, 64, 84
prepositions in 78
verbs in 76–77
sequence of ideas 52
session, plenary 38
settings of stories 55
Shakespeare, William 10–11, 20–21
short stories 65–66, 89
singular words 82–84
skim reading 50
slang 17
slogans 28, 32
sociology 49
sounds of letters 13
speaking 34
  at interview 40–41
speech 42, 45
  devices 28
  direct 56–57, 84–86
  figures of 28
  indirect 56–57, 60
  parts of 73
  reported 56
  scripted 56–57
speech marks (quotation marks) 56–57, 87
spell-checker 47, 54
spelling 47, 54, 79–84
  rules 82–84
spider diagram 42, 43
spoken word 16, 19, 41, 58, 80–81
Standard English 15, 18–19
statistics 26–27
stories 61
  title 60
  writing 55, 60, 61, 86
subheadings 52–53
subject of sentence 78–79
subordinate clauses 79, 85
suffixes 81–82
summary 38, 50, 55, 85
surface meaning 25, 28
syllables 79

T

Tales from Shakespeare 21

talk, preparing a 45
television 16, 41, 57
tense
  conditional 57
  future 57, 77
  past 57, 77
  present 57, 77
text, order of 50
text sampling 64
textbooks 49
theme 52
theory 52
thesaurus 48
title
  book 64–68, 84, 87
  film 87
  play 87
  story 60
tone 86
  of voice 41
  of written report 53
topic
  discussion 38
  for talk 45
toponyms 18

U

Ulysses 53

V

verbs 57, 76–79, 84
vocabulary 27
voice, tone of 41

W

Welsh language 11
Wilde, Oscar 10
word association 17, 27–28, 48
word–pictures 16
word processing 47, 55
words
  borrowed 11
  connected with church 12
  dialect 18
  English 10–23
  French 14
  Greek 13
  Latin 13, 16
  made-up 17

INDEX

meaning of 19, 28, 69, 81
new 16–17
non-Standard English 17
origins of 13
on posters 28
range of meaning of 47
scientific 13
shortening 81
spoken 19, 58, 80–81
written 19, 58
writing
 dialect 19
 dialogue 57
 experiments 53
 investigations 53
 lists 43
 minutes 35–37
 narrative 55
 notes 37, 42
 paragraphs 52
 process 53
 reports 41, 51, 53, 59, 87
 speeches 42
 Standard English 19
 stories 60, 86

Acknowledgements

Extract from *No Need for Heroes* by Brian Keaney on pp 70–71 reproduced with permission of Oxford University Press.
Poster on page 29 reproduced with permission of the Health Education Authority. © Copyright Health Education Authority.
Roget's Thesaurus on page 48, Longman Group Ltd.

Titles in *The Way to Pass* series

These books are available at £7.99 each from all good bookshops or directly from Vermilion (post and packing free) using the form below, or on our credit card hotline on **0279 427203.**

ORDER FORM

National Curriculum English

				Quantity
Level 4	Key Stage 3	11-14 years	0 09 178129 9	....
Level 5	Key Stage 3	11-14 years	0 09 178135 3	....
Level 6	Key Stage 3	11-14 years	0 09 178133 7	....
GCSE	Key Stage 4	14-16 years	0 09 178131 0	....

National Curriculum Maths

Level 4	Key Stage 3	11-14 years	0 09 178116 7	....
Level 5	Key Stage 3	11-14 years	0 09 178118 3	....
Level 6	Key Stage 3	11-14 years	0 09 178125 6	....
GCSE Foundation Level	Key Stage 4	14-16 years	0 09 178123 X	....
GCSE Intermediate Level	Key Stage 4	14-16 years	0 09 178121 3	....
GCSE Higher Level	Key Stage 4	14-16 years	0 09 178127 2	....

Mr/Ms/Mrs/Miss. ....

Address: ....

....

....

Postcode: .... Signed: ....

HOW TO PAY
I enclose cheque / postal order for £......... : ....made payable to VERMILION
I wish to pay by Access / Visa card (delete where appropriate)

Card No ....Expiry date: ....

Post order to **Murlyn Services Ltd, PO Box 50, Harlow, Essex CM17 ODZ.**

POSTAGE AND PACKING ARE FREE. Offer open in Great Britain including Northern Ireland. Books should arrive less than 28 days after we receive your order; they are subject to availability at time of ordering. If not entirely satisfied return in the same packaging and condition as received with a covering letter within 7 days. Vermilion books are available from all good booksellers

The Video Class Mathematics and *English* videos which accompany the above titles are available at £12.99 from leading video retailers and bookshops, or on the credit card hotline **0275 857017.**